Insights on Insincerity

Insights on Insincerity

How Educators Can Enhance the Classroom Experience

Chris Edwards

ROWMAN & LITTLEFIELD
Lanham • Boulder • New York • London

Published by Rowman & Littlefield
A wholly owned subsidiary of The Rowman & Littlefield Publishing Group, Inc.
4501 Forbes Boulevard, Suite 200, Lanham, Maryland 20706
www.rowman.com

Unit A, Whitacre Mews, 26-34 Stannary Street, London SE11 4AB

Copyright © 2018 by Rowman & Littlefield

All rights reserved. No part of this book may be reproduced in any form or by any electronic or mechanical means, including information storage and retrieval systems, without written permission from the publisher, except by a reviewer who may quote passages in a review.

British Library Cataloguing in Publication Information Available

Library of Congress Cataloging-in-Publication Data Available
Library of Congress Control Number: 2018933970

ISBN 978-1-4758-4171-8 (cloth : alk. paper)
ISBN 978-1-4758-4172-5 (pbk. : alk. paper)
ISBN 978-1-4758-4173-2 (electronic)

∞ ™ The paper used in this publication meets the minimum requirements of American National Standard for Information Sciences Permanence of Paper for Printed Library Materials, ANSI/NISO Z39.48-1992.

Printed in the United States of America

For the brave men and women on the Pulitzer Prize committee for Non-fiction writing. Also, this is for the handsome folks who pick the Nobel Prize winner for Literature every year.

Contents

Preface	ix
Acknowledgments	xiii
Introduction	xv
1 Insincerity from Authority	1
2 Insincerity from the Subordinate	25
3 Insincerity among Equals	57
4 Insincerity in Society and with the Self	83
Conclusion	99
References	103
About the Author	107

Preface

My Gmail account now offers me four or five different canned responses, based on some word-recognition algorithm, that I can choose to send when I receive e-mails. I can now click only one button and send a "Wow, thanks!" or some variation to someone, in response to just about any message. These responses exist because, for people who receive more correspondence than I do, the act of responding to e-mails has become a check-off-the-box exercise in pointlessness. Someone is sending a message only to say that a message has been sent, not to actually convey any information or make any connection between ideas.

Most of the time, insincerity manifests itself in these types of tedious human exchanges. Relationships require maintenance, and insincerity must suffice where true passion wanes. In the eighteenth and nineteenth centuries, during a time when the arrival of a message probably elicited excitement rather than fatigue, letter writers would try to outdo one another with flowery language.

One can still find the "Collected Letters" of various great academic and political figures from that era and see that the letter once counted as a literary form. Future historians will probably not edit, bind, and publish anything titled "Collected Tweets and Automatic Replies."

What does it mean to click on a reply that says "Wow, thanks!" while I sit, stone-faced, cycling through messages that I feel an obligation to reply to only for the purpose of holding up the thin veneer of a relationship? How would it be different if I simply set up a computer algorithm to reply to troublesome messages? What function does insincerity play in these interactions?

No specific incident made me want to write this book, but two different experiences, one specific and the other part of a general pattern, influenced my thinking. The specific incident occurred a number of years ago when, during a mid-week day off, I took my then-four-year-old youngest son to a restaurant that promises country cookin'. On that day, I had a newspaper with me, and after we ordered, I left it on the table while I took my son to the restroom.

When we returned, my waitress appeared sincerely distressed. The man who buses the tables had mistakenly thrown my newspaper away. I assured my waitress that not only did the newspaper represent no significant loss but that not having to read the daily list of horrors in the paper probably would make my day better. She remained unconvinced, and not only did she apologize profusely but also the man who bussed the tables came out of the back and told me he was sorry.

At the end of the meal, the waitress presented my son and me with a box of free cookies to make up for the newspaper. One does not refuse a box of free cookies, especially not when they are presented in front of a four-year-old, but at that point I wondered what caused such severe distress on the part of these poor people working in the restaurant. Bankers, corporate bureaucrats, and federal politicians rip me off all the time *on purpose* and none of them ever brings me a box of cookies. These nice working people simply made a mistake involving something that was about to be thrown away anyway, and they felt the need to make amends.

This got me to thinking that perhaps sincerity holds Western civilization together. How many people go to work and sincerely try to do a good job? How much gets accomplished because police officers, teachers, auto mechanics, insurance adjustors, and locally elected political figures simply try to do their jobs well? Occasionally, I read something in my local newspaper that reaffirms this view.

The town council in the little Midwestern community where I live recently paid a company to review the sewer system. That company determined that the sewers would only last a few more years without repair. The town council put aside funds to make the preemptive repairs and then issued a very modest tax increase to the town's residents to pay for the repairs. Try to explain how something so boringly competent happened without assuming that everyone involved just sincerely wanted to do a good job.

My general experiences with insincerity usually come whenever I encounter some type of corporate hierarchy that seems to exist for no other reason than to perpetuate its own existence. Yet, for whatever reason, when the people in the hierarchy really just want to force mandates on people who are lower down, the process gets dressed up as a "consensus building."

Whenever someone who occupies a lower hierarchical rung actually tries to make an argument for change, he will likely receive the statement that fully embodies societal insincerity: "Thanks so much for your feedback." What this means, really, is that the purpose of soliciting advice or suggestions from you was really just to let you think you had some input, when the corporate hierarchs had long ago decided on a course of action.

No romantic poet ever conjured up a more beautiful phrase than "meeting canceled," and this is because meetings almost uniformly waste time in insincere displays of intra-corporate politicking. Yet, it certainly cannot be said that insincerity provides no useful function to society. In fact, as this book will argue, insincerity is one of the key factors of human interaction and, therefore, anyone who seeks to study the humanities would do well to analyze how insincerity shapes literature, history, psychology, and sociology.

I have no desire to create a school of "insincerity studies," but the more I thought about sincerity and insincerity, the more it shaped not only the way I read literature and studied history but also how I interacted with colleagues and acquaintances. Some general rules of human interaction can be discerned. For example, you can usually judge how insincere you are expected to behave for an event by how well you must dress for it.

We now live in a society that increasingly embraces insincerity as a medium of exchange, where one can reply to human correspondence with a computer-generated response and place only good news and smiling faces on social media. The concept of insincerity, too long ignored, should be better studied and more frequently taught. Hopefully, this book will provide the first attempt to analyze this important factor of human interchange.

Acknowledgments

Thanks, as always, to Tom Koerner for his guidance, professionalism, and editorial expertise. All writers should be so lucky as to have an editor like Tom. Thanks to my wife, Beth, who has pretended to like me for over twenty years and has done a pretty good job of it. My sons, both of them masters of flattery, deserve love and thanks for what they have taught me.

Introduction

Everyone leaves the meeting wondering what it was for. Nothing important was accomplished, no new insights were shared, the "leadership team" or whatever the local euphemism for middle management is, simply passed around a microphone and read off information that would have been more efficiently shared through an e-mail.

The unfortunates who sat through the meeting will spend a good deal of the rest of the day sharing complaints with one another about how the meeting took up mental energy that could have been spent on other tasks that hold more value for the corporation. The subordinates sing an angry refrain that the meeting was a pointless waste of time. But it wasn't. The stated purpose of the meeting just did not align with the real purpose. Most meetings are insincerity made manifest.

The truly fascinating thing about insincerity has to do with the fact that it can only exist when an encounter among people contains a stated and unstated purpose. The stated purpose may be the ostensible reason for the encounter, but the real purpose remains unstated, felt but not defined. The stated purpose of the hypothetical meeting may have been to convey information and to initiate feedback. The management hid an unstated, and primary, purpose under the power-points and slogans: reinforcement of the hierarchy.

Lower-ranking members of the hierarchy must sit and listen to the vision and to the information. The higher-ranking members of the hierarchy might even pass around a sound-amplifying device, often a phallic symbol, while expecting to see reactions from the peons; heads nod, eyes up front, and with a suitably subservient facial expression.

Most meetings are examples of how insincerity gets expressed from authority downward. Unfortunately, when authority practices a ritual of insincerity, such as a meeting, the ritual often includes some variation of "team building." This forces the subordinates to act one way (happy) while feeling another (humiliated), thus building insincerity into the corporate culture.

The word *insincerity* means to act one way but to feel another and is usually used to describe individual behavior, but it can be manifested in organizations and cultures at a larger level. There is no exact synonym for the word. *Hypocrisy*, for example, means to say one thing and do another. Insincerity can be expressed through four types of relationships: (1) from authority to subordinate, (2) from a subordinate to authority, (3) between equals, and (4) to oneself and in society.

Team-building exercises sometimes get labeled as "forced fun," and while the stated purpose is "team building," the unstated purpose is to control. Management has decreed fun time, and to refuse that fun time is to refuse to be a "team player." Why is being a team player ranked more highly than being a productive loner? Only team players fit into the hierarchy and, therefore, play into the unstated management goal for the meeting.

Consider this passage from the wonderful *Getting Schooled: The Reeducation of an American Teacher* by Garret Keizer. Keizer gave up teaching English in a public school in favor of being a writer and a parent (being even two of the three stretches one's limits) and then returned to the classroom to cover for a maternity leave and to gain the elusive insurance coverage. On one of his first days back as a teacher, he found himself enduring a staff-wide team-building experience titled "Let the Games Begin."

Keizer writes that this "gives me pause. I tell myself it is probably a metaphor, something like 'play ball' or 'to your marks, get set, go,' and completely in keeping with the athletic sensibilities of our administration . . . I ought to know better" (2014, 41–42).

Keizer and the rest of the staff get a lecture about how important it can be to play with the team and to engage in the same kind of uncomfortable activities that students can be asked to do. Keizer:

> It is acting like a prima donna that I fear the most and so I resolve that I am going to play along, though I will never in the course of the year feel more tempted to walk out of the building than I do right then. Without going into tedious detail, the game is basically a treasure hunt that each team of tablemates is to conduct while holding on to a length of clothesline. Since this is a timed race, it behooves each team to move quickly, which is to say, as quickly as its slowest member allows. Since the clues are scattered throughout the school and over the sprawling school grounds, and since I have spent the last weeks of the summer taking medication for an injury to my feet, it does not take long for me to be in some pain. It takes even less time for me to feel humiliated. Well, Garrett, this is what *work* means for most people . . . (2014, 42)

Forced fun combines dictatorial control enforced on individuals who fear being viewed by peers as a "prima donna." Nothing offends authority like dignity among the subordinates. These team-building games, like all games, substitute for a lack of purpose or vision. For half-literate middle managers, the games also serve a function similar to that of a tuxedo for a formal event; there must be comfort in looking around and seeing that one is doing the same as everyone else.

This kind of stuff is in the marrow of American culture. One of the greatest ironies about "Little League" baseball, on display on every field in every rink-a-dink town and strip-malled suburb in the country is that the siblings of the baseball players always have more fun than the kids on the field. The stated point is for the players to have fun, but the real purpose is to give dads an outlet for their talk-radio fantasies. Every middle-aged dad with "COACH" stenciled on his back underneath an ad for the local mortuary or ice-cream and slop shop keeps a running third-person commentary in his mind.

Meanwhile, the brothers and sisters of the kids on the field find they have a marvelous little reprieve from the watchful eyes of out-of-control adults. They then sprint up and down dirt mounds, play catch, or find the rewards in just running around and trying to tag one another. Look around one day at your local children's sporting event. The siblings run around playing tag and giggling. The kids on the field stand in some kind of military formation, trying to remember whatever arbitrary rules that must be followed.

If the real purpose of the games is to let the kids have fun, then why not just agree to show up somewhere and let the kids play with other kids for a couple of hours? The reason is that there is nothing in this for the adults who would have to drive the kids there.

For the subordinate, constant contact with insincerity leads eventually to cynicism, the assurance that every corporate gathering, committee meeting, and staff training exists for an insincere purpose. The slightly hidden nature of these small humiliations makes self-deception possible; the lacerations accumulate, until ultimately one is standing in a red pool of one's former self-respect. You'll accept these humiliations because you do not believe that you possess the talent to engage in the kind of work that would allow you to avoid them. That's sincere.

The word *insincerity* carries with it connotations of sliminess, as if the purpose of acting another way than one feels is ultimately an act of dishonesty and manipulation. However, a mother who buries her grief so she will not traumatize her children with a show of painful emotion acts insincerely just as much as the Iranian government does when proclaiming that their nuclear program exists only for energy purposes.

Insincerity, as an art, can be practiced by subordinates as well but usually with negative effects. Subordinates who detect insincerity from the power structure. "Thanks *so* much . . ." can do little but shove down the frustration and pressurize it into bile. Authority figures who detect insincerity in subordinates, however, can block opportunities, fail to communicate, and frustrate ambitions. Only in cases where the subordinates need nothing and fear nothing from their authorities can they practice insincerity in a muscular way.

Meanwhile, sincerity itself remains the province of only a few, to be exercised by those who are either so far at the bottom of a social hierarchy that they need not fear being reproached (custodians need not suffer through any team-building exercises) or by those at the top of the hierarchies. An entire industry feeds into the Insincerity business, with corporate consultants advising managers in the best way to manipulate the middle managers; so *many* ways to force a frozen smile onto the faces of those who spend their days punching in data and generating reports. Subordinates may express insincerity to authority (when it becomes deliberately visible, we call it sarcasm) but must do so with a greater level of expertise.

Insincerity can be positive; adults must sometimes feign excitement over the LEGO creations or blobbish scribbles of toddlers. In some cases, insincerity itself acts as a direct medium of exchange, usually when practiced among equals. No one in a romantic relationship should take the words "I'm fine" literally from a crying partner. Yet, by and large the consistent effect of tolerating and perpetuating insincerity is likely a diminishing of oneself, a poisoning of the emotional bloodstream through frustration.

Ultimately, a person can become insincere with herself, usually as a form of psychological protection. This insight belongs to Freud, and became the basis for psychology in the late nineteenth century. Freud's focus on individual insincerity may have prevented him, and subsequent psychologists who have studied authority, from seeing the sincere connections between relationships and insincerity.

The ephemeral nature of insincerity means it exists precisely because it can be denied. This prevents it from being measurable through scientific means of analysis. Please do not read this as a work of science but, rather, one of cultural analysis. Scientific evidence will play a part where applicable, but for the most part, trying to measure insincerity scientifically is like trying to capture fog in a glass beaker to take it back to a lab.

Also, books with a too-formal chapter/content structure assume a level of semi-literacy from readers that becomes tiresome and even insulting. Hopefully, this work will not fit well on the shelves with the single-word-and-some-examples type of nonfiction books that too often make it to the bestseller lists because they can be understood by reading the book jacket. The structure here is loose and the content conversational, which means it will be arranged by the connections through the content and understood through the four relationships in which it gets expressed, not through a progressive chapter arrangement.

Insincerity, fundamental to the human social experience, connects psychology, politics, religion, and literature. Skeptics need not worry; no attempts will be made here to connect insincerity with any of the hard sciences. No argument will be made here that quantum particles act insincerely when they show their position but hide their velocity. That being said, my primary academic interest is in the burgeoning new field of studying and creating cross-curricular connections and hope that this book will be seen as a contribution to that field of practice.

This, more than anything, is why the book is written for professors and teachers as well as a lay audience. Professors who study only in one field might miss lines of connections among other fields, and these connections create pictures that add insight to our studies. This is the purpose, after all, of the humanities. This book references both Great Books and popular culture because an effective teaching technique often begins by having students develop an understanding of something they are familiar with and then transferring that understanding to something they are not.

The purpose of this book is to explore insincerity's impact on cultural studies, and the closest analogy might be to feminist studies. In the past, feminist historians and literary critics drew attention to the female experience in culture and reshaped the way in which academics viewed critical texts. From this came the concept of feminist history and literary critique, or what might more broadly be defined as gender studies.

Feminist studies, much maligned by the just-teach-engineering crowd, forced a new viewpoint into university cultural studies programs. The study of gender roles in culture developed a new perspective that led to a greater understanding of the initial texts. Harold Bloom, the great literary critic, sometimes refers to the feminist and minority viewpoint on cultural studies as a "school of resentment."

Feminist studies may have evolved into that, and all big ideas must be pushed forward with some force of anger at the establishment, but the concept of studying culture with a view toward new insights should not be confused or correlated with resentment at all culture. Properly done, feminist studies should deepen our understanding and appreciation for the traditional canon while creating room for new additions.

Ultimately, the purpose of any book for educators of the humanities or social studies is to analyze a previously unrecognized aspect of literature, history, and human interactions so that the classroom experience might be enhanced. To that end, the contention of this book is that insincerity remains underappreciated as a cultural force in the same way that the female experience in history and literature was at one time.

Furthermore, a failure to analyze insincerity properly has caused serious misunderstandings of the concept to develop. Eric Blair, also known as George Orwell, positioned himself as the great definer of insincerity in politics and literature. But he got the concept wrong in *1984* (1949) and mangled the analysis of insincerity in politics for subsequent generations. An analysis of *1984* helps to clear up misconceptions about insincerity to political power, and these insights might be valuable not just for the classroom but also for political analysis.

The purpose of this book is not to draw attention to a human perspective, as feminist studies did, but to analyze the importance of a particular kind of human interaction as it exists across disciplines. To that end, the closest antecedent to this book is Erving Goffman's 1956 classic *The Presentation of Self in Everyday Life*.

While not about insincerity, Goffman's work analyzed a variety of human interactions through the analogy of the stage play and used this single conceit to clarify the actions of human beings in a variety of experiences. Something similar will be attempted here in the sense that any time a professor or teacher can connect a type of human interaction inherent in Greek literature or romanticism with the same type of interaction as it exists in modern culture, then one deepens the interest of students in both. Of course, there likely will be objections to the analyses put forth here. This is fine because the best thing about writing a book like this, probably, is that it provides a ready-made response to any criticism. You can probably guess what that will be:

Thanks so much for your feedback.

Chapter One

Insincerity from Authority

Ethical considerations for experimental subjects hinder the impact of modern psychology to a great degree. In fact, most of what we understand about human nature must be derived from now decades-old experiments such as those performed by Yale professor Stanley Milgram in the 1960s. The experiment that Milgram and his associates performed now resides in the cultural memory, so only a few words of description will be used here. Insincerity resides at the core of these experiments. Unknowing individuals who thought they were signing up to help in a medical/psychological experiment actually ended up being the test subjects themselves.

The setup and results of these experiments are well known. An unknowing individual came into a lab where an actor posing as a doctor in a white lab coat ordered the individual to turn a dial that sent electric shocks into a person sitting in another room. The person in the other room, another actor, pretended to be hurt, because the electric shocks did not really exist.

To sum up the results, most people followed authority pretty far. The purpose here is not to rehash theories about authority. The purpose here is to point out the central place of insincerity in the Milgram experiments. For the unknowing volunteers who walked into the trap that Milgram had set, the purpose of the experiments was to help administer electric shocks (but not really) on people in another room.

The unstated purpose, however, was to test the "volunteers" since they believed the faked shocks to be real. At one level, Milgram's experiment might be seen as an experiment in how far people will follow authority. At another level, it can be seen as an experiment in how well people detect insincerity.

One hundred percent of volunteers failed to detect the insincerity behind the program. Most people delivered the shocks, some delivered them for a very long time at a very high level, but no one stood up and said, "This whole thing is a setup." In fact, the entire field of psychology might be understood as the study of the insincere, in that Freud believed that people hid their natures and feelings to such a great extent that it caused self-deception and psychosis, but a more in-depth analysis of this point will have to wait for a few chapters.

An experiment like Milgram's would not be possible in modern psychology because of serious ethical concerns; the volunteers did not extend any kind of informed consent. The concept of "informed consent" destroys any kind of interesting psychological experiments because you cannot consent to being tricked any more than you can tickle yourself. The consent form tips the test subject off that he or she is about to be thrust into an environment of the insincere and therefore will inevitably put that person on the high defensive. Insincerity depends upon deception.

It should be pointed out that Milgram is no guiltier of unethical behavior than the God of the Bible. God is, as Harold Bloom always notes, a literary character and a fascinating one at that. Has there ever been a literary figure less sincere than the Judeo-Christian-Islamic God?

God never wanted the Garden of Eden to last, otherwise no tree of knowledge would have twisted its way up through the soil. Why did the fruit taste so good in the first place? The whole thing was a setup. Satan, at least, hisses a sincere hymn to Eve. Nothing can be sincerer than temptation; drug addicts and alcoholics tremble with sincerity and only become sick when they are insincere. Satan tempts; he wants Eve to do exactly what he says he wants her to do. "Taste the fruit, Eve," he hisses, and she does. He wanted from her exactly what he said he wanted. Eve then tempts Adam in the same direct way.

Enter God with his theatrical rage. He banishes the couple and curses the uteri of every woman who will follow Eve with the pain of childbirth (a head-scratcher, that one, unless the theocrats who authored Genesis had gotten enough "what the heck is up with this?" inquiries from people who had watched women giving birth) and then sends angels to guard the Garden of Eden.

The Old Testament records nothing about God punishing the serpent-as-Satan. Please hold on to that point as it will apply shortly in an analysis of the Book of Job and how it relates to the views of Jesus regarding insincerity. God loves insincere experiments. After Adam and Eve, the next time the reader encounters him, he's messing with his most sincere follower, Abraham.

Biblical scholars, both devout and secular, have been analyzing the curious Genesis story of God, Abraham, and Isaac ever since the ink first dried on it and probably even before that when the story was written in the sound waves of Hebrew bards. Abraham, the biblical founder of monotheism, receives an intense order from his Lord: *kill your son as a show of devotion to me*. Thus God commanded.

Abraham must have employed insincerity to lure his boy, the adolescent Isaac, up to a quiet place with an altar for devotional execution. Genesis records no incident of struggle. What, we may wonder, did Abraham say to get Isaac to stretch out on the altar? Presumably, as an altar of sacrifice, Isaac would have seen what happened to all sorts of animals there. Did Abraham say, "Hey son, you look tired, why not stretch out on the old blood-stained altar over there and have a nap while I scrounge around for some berries?"

At any rate, the scene is set with Isaac lying on the altar. Then, just as Abraham raises the knife above his boy, a crackling noise reaches his ear from a nearby thicket. Abraham sees a ram with his horns caught in the bushes and realizes that this is God's way of yelling, "Pysche! I was just kidding, kill this ram instead." (The ram got set up here, too, by the way.) Abraham had proved his sincere faith in God's word by preparing to murder his son on God's orders, and as a reward, he did not actually have to murder his own son.

Is one allowed to raise one's hand during a sermon? A few questions come to mind, here. Number one: God gives the whole "kill your son because I said so," order quite clearly. The words seem to come from the otherworld that God inhabits. Yet, the "just kidding, you don't have to kill your son, massacre this animal instead," order gets delivered rather indirectly. Abraham must assume that the ram is an alternative sacrifice. Surely rams get caught in thickets sometimes; maybe this was a coincidence and Abraham misread the situation?

What if God looked down later and said "you killed what now? No, no, no, I wanted you to kill Isaac not some clumsy ram. Where did you get that idea?" Even if God did intend for the ram to be an alternative sacrifice, why is he counting on Abraham's ability to infer this? Abraham would seem to be rather immune to subtlety. Of course, a believer might simply say that God controlled the whole thing supernaturally, but that would void the purpose of the experiment. The unknown factor here, and the reason for God's insincerity, is Abraham's level of faith and obedience.

Scholars read this story as an example of the biblical injunction to be totally obedient to God. Total obedience will be rewarded over time in the way that God chooses, even if the reward is simply not having to engage in the truly heinous act that God had originally ordered. Yet, the story of God, Abraham, and Isaac reveals God as a manifestation of insincerity. He never intended for Abraham to kill his son; that was the stated purpose. The unstated purpose was to test Abraham's faith in a Milgram-like psychological experiment. Abraham, likewise, tricks Isaac with insincerity, and this reveals that insincerity is the province of authority. It is okay to use only on subordinates.

This connects with a common biblical theme. Before the story of Abraham and Isaac, Adam and Eve lied to God about eating from the Tree of Knowledge. They received punishment for their insincere response. Then, the couple had two sons named Cain and Abel. Cain killed Abel in a sincere act of murder but then lied to God about it and suffered punishment. God may employ insincerity from the top down, and he would apparently tolerate insincerity from middle managers like Satan or Abraham as long as it was aimed at their subordinates; just don't try to be insincere from the bottom up. Was that the real sin?

Oh, there's more. Later, in the Book of Job, God and Satan casually chat up a bet about God's favorite servant, Job. God lets the devil torment Job to test the man's faith. Poor Job sees this as a sincere punishment for him and sincerely takes everything thrown at him but never pretends not to feel the pain.

Job wails and cries about his condition, but if he wanted to curse God as his wife told him to, he kept that part to himself. Eventually, God reins in the devil and, apparently in a more expansive mood toward Job than he had been toward Abraham, gives him some pretty great consolation gifts to make up for everything that had been taken from him.

Maybe this is better; maybe it is not. If God had treated Abraham like he had treated Job, then Abraham would have plunged the knife into the heart of his son but then would have been given a new and better son later. Nonetheless, Job suffers the punishment, but Satan, again, seems cleared. He was the agent here of God's insincere test, not a freelancer, and freelancing seems to be the real sin.

The Bible cannot be read as a book because it is a collection of books, an anthology of ancient texts. Religious scholars who try to connect the separate books into a coherent narrative tend to do so by highlighting Old Testament prophecies regarding a savior and see the New Testament as evidence of the prophecy's fulfillment.

This logic contains and internal consistency only among an audience that views the Old and New Testaments as historical works rather than literary. For skeptics, the arrival of Jesus as a fulfillment of Old Testament prophecy reveals nothing but the fact that the authors of the New Testament works (whomever they were) had the Old Testament close at hand and, therefore, could write the story of Jesus so that it aligned with previous prophecies. The fact that Jesus "fulfilled" Old Testament prophecy appears to be no more significant than the fact that Harry Potter or Luke Skywalker fulfilled their destinies in alignment with what previous episodes or books predicted.

The reason this becomes pertinent for a discussion of insincerity has to do with the message of Jesus regarding insincerity. In Matthew 6:5, he commands his followers with this phrase:

> And when you pray, do not be like the hypocrites, for they love to pray standing in the synagogues and on the street corners to be seen by others. Truly I tell you, they have received their reward in full.

What does that mean? Praying in public would not make a person a hypocrite. Hypocrisy is the act of doing one thing while saying another. Is this a poor translation from the Greek? *Hypocrite* is about as Greek a word as it gets; and the term apparently translates best into "stage actor." In other words, the intent of the public prayers seems to be to put on a show. People who pray in public, therefore, should be described as insincere. Jesus indicates that the public display of prayer would make it a more insincere show.

The Hypocrites apparently want to be seen as holy men, and so they pray in public not for the purpose of expressing real faith, but for the purpose of enhancing their reputations among the people. Insincerity deteriorates the power of their real faith.

Jesus declares private prayer to be more sincere than public prayer and extolls his followers to pray sincerely and quietly. From this likely comes the notion, prevalent for some reason, that those who keep charitable contributions quiet act in a way that has greater sincerity and therefore a greater level of altruism.

Larry David lampooned this notion in an episode of *Curb Your Enthusiasm* titled "The Private Donor." Larry gave money publicly while his friend Ted Danson did so privately. Everyone knew, however, that Ted gave the money, but this public "secret" only enhanced Ted Danson's reputation among everyone. Much to David's chagrin, Danson got double credit for his contribution: one for giving the money and another for doing it as a private donor.

Why would privacy equal sincerity? It does not, necessarily, but the fact that most people attribute quiet altruism to a greater level of sincerity speaks to the power of insincerity. For the powerful, the great thing about insincerity comes from its very unprovability; managers who send out congratulatory e-mails to the whole staff or to all employees do so knowing that no spirits will be lifted but that appearances will be kept up. What, though, can the subordinate say? "He didn't mean it when he wrote 'great job, team!'" What subordinate dares suggest that one-way praise amounts to a form of condescension and control?

Christianity praises sincerity, but God made liberal use of insincerity from his middle managers and seemed unbothered by it unless it was aimed upward. The groveling Christians are made up of slaves, prostitutes, and anyone else at the bottom of the hierarchy. Only they are truly sincere and, therefore, shall inherit the Earth. Only they never do. Jesus told people to pray in secret yet preached on a hillside; he was insincerity incarnate. Then he died in a big show, but not really. The stated purpose for the crucifixion involved an execution, but the hidden purpose was the resurrection.

The focus of Greek literature and mythology tended to be about the dangers of *hubris* and *nemesis*. Success creates arrogance, arrogance leads to bad decision making, and bad decision making then leads to the fall. If anything is insincere in Greek literature, it must be the character of prophecy. Characters are informed of the future only so they can be given the illusion that they can change it.

For Socrates, the "good life" amounted to a sincere life. He said what he felt, asked the questions he wanted, tweaked the powers-at-be with his wit, and lived like a free man because of it. Old men who maintain their idealism will always attract the peach-fuzzed youth, but Socrates made few friends among his peers. Sincerity caused a happy death; he drank the Hemlock in good cheer and without crossing his fingers behind his back as Jesus would later do. Unlike the case of Jesus, death actually ended the life of Socrates, and he lives on only through philosophy.

The word *cynic*, Greek of course, means "dog." Cynicism comes about as a result of too much contact with insincerity, and the Cynics decided to avoid the whole insincere mess of society by simply living dog-like in the streets. Diogenes, the most famous of the Cynics, lived during the time of Alexander the Great in the fourth century BC. The famous story involving Diogenes has him lying on his back and sunning himself when the shade of Alexander's standing figure fell upon him.

"Diogenes, I will give you whatever you want," said Alexander.

Comic timing being essential for any Cynic, Diogenes responded with, "I'd like you get to get out of my sun."

Alexander said that if he could not be himself he would be Diogenes and the homeless man returned the compliment. Insincerity could only be avoided at the bottom and top of the hierarchy, and the Greek philosophers often extolled the virtues of being on one end or the other while avoiding the middle.

Diogenes was an Athenian, though, and Athenians seemed to prefer sincerity to its opposite. The Spartans held different views. In his classic book *On Sparta*, Plutarch writes of how young Spartan commanders, called *Eirens*, toughened the boys under his control with the *agoge* training/educational system:

> So such an Eiren, twenty years of age, commands those under him in his Troop's fights, while in his quarters he has them serve him his meals like servants. The burlier boys he instructs to bring wood, the slighter ones to collect vegetables. They steal what they fetch, some of them entering gardens, others slipping into the men's messes with a fine mixture of cunning and caution. If a boy is caught, he receives many lashes of the whip for proving to be a clumsy, unskilled thief. The boys also steal whatever provisions they can,

thereby learning how to pounce skillfully upon those who are asleep or keeping guard carelessly. A boy is beaten and goes hungry if he is caught. The aim of providing them with only sparse fare is that they should be driven to make up its deficiencies by resort to daring and villainy. (1988 [reprint], 22)

The Spartan commanders outlawed "villainy" and punished the boys for being caught. The whole training system for the famous Spartans centered on insincerity. The controlling powers created a setup for the boys in training that, on the surface, looked like an educational and training structure. Starving the boys until they had no recourse except to steal, the real purpose, never got stated. One can imagine that the less cynical children who never figured this out died out in this environment.

Then Plutarch relates just how seriously the students took their insincerity:

> The care which the boys take over their stealing is illustrated by the story of the one who had stolen a fox cub and had it concealed inside his cloak: in order to escape detection he was prepared to have his insides clawed and bitten out by the animal and even to die. This tale is certainly not incredible, judging from Spartan ephebes today. I have witnessed many of them dying under the lashes they received at the altar of Artemis Orthia. (1988 [reprint], 23)

If the definition of *insincerity* involves masking one's true feelings, then surely this unnamed Spartan boy, even if he likely does qualify as apocryphal, wins some sort of blue ribbon for his efforts. Not wanting to be caught in the act of stealing a fox (are these good eating?), he keeps a stone face while the animal clawed out his innards. Bravo!

The Spartans staked their entire society on training their warriors to deny the effects of fear and privation, and to act stoically when surely their emotions and thoughts encouraged them to run away from the pointy things being either shot or thrust into their direction. Over time, however, the goal must have been to make the insincere sincere, to actually change the inner character of the warrior to the point where he craved the challenges.

This makes it difficult to define whether the Spartan boy qualifies as a subordinate or not. His inclusion in this chapter on insincerity and authority, rather than on the next about insincerity and the subordinate, has to do with the fact that the boy apparently acted of his own accord. The point of the story of the Spartan boy and the fox hardly seems to be that "students" of the Spartan system lived so much in fear of their masters' discipline that they would suffer a painful death rather than suffer punishment.

Yet, what punishment could be worse than feeling the needle-like claws and gnawing teeth of the fox in your intestines? The point seems to be that this boy mastered himself, and chose to die rather than to face the humiliation of being caught. This is not a child frightened of being in trouble, but a man who made a choice: this may have been what the insincere Spartan system of education hoped to produce.

Again, *hypocrite* means "stage actor," and no one must act more effectively and therefore more insincerely than a prostitute. Strippers, literal stage actors, put a commodity on insincerity. Tuck a dollar and they will pretend to like you, whomever you are. Men and women willingly line up for the purpose of being fooled. Flattery and sexual temptation usually hang in the closet of psychological costumes employed by the subordinate, particularly women. Only occasionally does a temptress manage to become an empress, as was the case with the Byzantine empress Theodora, wife of the notable Justinian.

We shall learn of the most insincere of Byzantine bureaucrats, Procopius, in the next chapter. A subordinate, he practiced the tools of flattery to the royal faces but took a revenge of sorts, by keeping a Secret History about Emperor Justinian and Empress Theodora. The poison of suppressed rage, a poison only subordinates swallow, flowed from his pen and eventually into the pages of history. He wrote that Theodora slept her way into a theater career, then let the emperor Justinian relieve himself in an eye-rolling bout of exertion between her thighs. Seduced, he married her, and Theodora took the prefix of "Empress."

From the historical record, she doesn't seem so bad. Born in the year 500, she had given birth to a daughter and given up the life of a stage vixen by the year 525 when a transfixed Justinian discovered her at court and married her. She then assumed the powers of an empress. In those dreary days before the advent of NASCAR, slack-jawed subjects who wanted to watch a vehicle go around in a circle had to settle for horses and chariots. Spectators, forced to watch racing in an era before six-packs of beer and buckets of fried chicken, enjoyed themselves as best they could at the Hippodrome in the Byzantine capital of Constantinople.

In this bygone era, fans of racing teams donned a special color as a way of publicly showing their support for racing teams. The two major racing teams went by the color-affiliated titles of the "Blues" and the "Greens." All politicians at all times (including and especially university presidents) must grovel before the local sports franchise, and Justinian dutifully supported the Blues. Supporters of the teams tended to combine the worst aspects of spectatorship—being both blindingly devoted to whatever arbitrary side they had chosen to support and willing to defend the honor of their chariot racers through blunt force.

In 532, fanatic devotion morphed into a general riot, and the riot then turned into a political uprising. The Blues and the Greens combined forces and devoted their energies to trying to kill Justinian. This sort of thing happened in the Byzantine Empire with discomfiting regularity. The emperor might very well be a divinely inspired monarch, heir to Caesar and Constantine, but this held little truck for most of the bureaucrats and lower-caste royals who populated the court and propagated in one of the most poisonous political atmospheres of world history.

For some reason, political assassination tended to take the form of facial mutilation. More than a few Byzantine emperors suffered from having a nose sliced off, or from having the septum that separates the nostrils slit open with a knife. More frequently, emperors who lost favor got the old "eyes-scooped-out-with-a-knife" routine. Later, in the eighth century, Empress Irene ruled as a regent for her son until he came of age. When the boy got old enough to try and take over, Irene ordered her guards to hold her own son down and cut out his eyes. Infection or shock or some combination of both killed the boy not long after.

As a side note, history does make one wonder just how sincerely familial love is really felt in comparison to the desire for political power; Peter the Great and Suleyman the Magnificent both ordered the death of their own children, although at the risk of sounding sexist the whole child-killing-for-power bit does seem a bit worse coming from Mom. Anyway, when the Blues and Greens rose in rebellion, Justinian, no doubt with images of angry peasants with knives moving toward his face, showed an immediate predilection for running away.

Nothing shows more sincerity than the act of sprinting away from a scary situation in full terror mode. Leave it to a former prostitute to understand the danger of lifting a veil of insincerity at the wrong moment. Theodora told Justinian to swallow his fear and act like an emperor; she advised him to call in the military and slaughter the uppity Blues and Greens. Justinian, no genius according to Procopius, followed this good advice. Theodora kept her cool, and because of this, Justinian kept his eyes, nose, and head.

Procopius's nefarious portrayal of Theodora may betray a specific fear of female insincerity. The dark art of flattery comes in the form of the prostitute's wink, of the stripper's false smile, of the wife's fake moans of pleasure. Men of power who fall for this insincerity might feel a burst of manly pride, but the discovery of its falseness might result in rage. Women who master the spells and potions of insubordinate sincerity, and manage to wield those arts so successfully that they find themselves in a position of power, must be dangerous indeed.

Enter Wu Zetian, a Chinese concubine whose beauty pulled her into the court of the Tang Dynasty. Born in 624, she must have flowered into an impressive looking young woman because the empire's scouts (men who plucked young beauties from the villages to be brought back into the bedroom of the emperor, either as brides or sex slaves) discovered her and took her to the royal palace.

One can only imagine the psychological impact that such actions had on a pubescent girl. What was it like to be taken from one's home and family, and then to arrive at the ornate court of the Tang, and then to find that you are there to perform sexual functions that you may not have been aware even existed?

The stories about Wu create an image of a Machiavellian temptress, one who flattered her way in the heart of the emperor while performing acts of murder that removed rival women from power. A few words should be added here about the curious nature of the emperor's court. In this era before DNA testing and daytime talk shows (the prince's *real* father is . . .), any man who worked at the imperial court must be castrated. Yes, this meant the taking of the frank and the beans.

The surgical details need not be detailed here, but you are probably curious, so why not? Someone sliced off the man's penis and testicles and then used a glass plug to keep the gaping and bloody hole open. After a few days of healing, if the man (former man? Cisgender person?) could squat and piss he would likely live. If not, the infection typically killed. In hard times, some men reportedly castrated themselves prior to asking for a job; this would seem to heighten the pain of rejection.

There could only be one penis swinging in the imperial palace; the mandate of heaven could only be passed on through the royal bloodlines. Whispers could hurt worse than arrows. Any hint of illegitimacy regarding the blood heritage of a prince could lead to the kind of doubts that create revolutions. The only way of assuring that the emperor's child really was the emperor's child was to make sure that the emperor was the only one capable of making a child.

In addition, the imperial castrates, called eunuchs, needed to be reminded that their job was to advise the emperor. By removing the penis and testes, one also removed perhaps the most serious distraction a man can have from his duties. This also functioned in the same way that celibacy, theoretically, did among the Catholic priests; it prevented the eunuchs from having children and therefore eliminated the desire to turn their positions into a hereditary caste. It also meant that priests and eunuchs could not pass on their property to a child, and so wealth reverted to the church or empire.

In this environment, a woman could rise from sex slave to regent of the empire if she could catch the seed of the emperor in her uterus. In this era of high child mortality, the purpose of the harem (well, the *stated* purpose) was to produce many heirs to the empire. A woman who gave birth to a child who would one day clutch the Mandate of Heaven could exercise her motherly authority over the emperor and therefore the empire.

Or, as was the case with Wu, a woman of means and wile could dominate a passive emperor. It's hard to imagine what kind of people that a pampered imperial lifestyle would create. What's it like to never be challenged and to have one's every whim satisfied by sycophantic eunuchs and advisors who hope to build a relationship with a child that will last into adulthood?

The court of China's imperial dynasties rank among the most insincere environments in world history. The point of the whole system, one supposes, had to have been to give the emperor the appearance of power with the real purpose being to create someone so stupid and placid that the imperial bureaucrats could exercise real governing authority.

Wu surely smiled while standing before, and moaned while lying under, the emperor but she showed the teeth of a Chinese dragon when vying for power with her fellow consorts. She smothered the baby of a rival to remove the infant from the chain of power. She positioned her own child as the heir to the Mandate. Even the method of killing, suffocation, speaks of the dark arts of female assassination—women preferred poison and pillows to axes and arrows. Wu could also, apparently, be more direct. She was said to have had one rival killed and made her into a fleshy meal for pigs.

Buddhism might have played a role in developing Wu's confidence. Buddhism favored an unorthodox approach to achieving a state of mind, and Buddhists tend to avoid doctrine. The Buddha, however, supposedly said some suspiciously antihierarchical aphorisms in his life, and this fit less than well next to the Tang Dynasty's guiding philosophy of Confucianism. Hierarchy was the stated goal of Confucius, who taught that society could only attain peace through the imposition of social stratification. Confucianism, and thus Chinese imperialist philosophy, can be summarized thusly: (a) the father is the head of the family; (b) the emperor is the head of China; and (c) China is the head of the world.

Wu shed her insincerity as she aged and asserted more power, eventually declaring herself empress through deed if not decree by taking over some of the ritualized rites of the emperor. Power sometimes causes one to lose proficiency in the arts of insincerity. As an old woman, she took two handsome young men, twins, as her lovers. Lechery can be forgiven in men of power, but never in women of power, and she lost her authority when her subordinates lost their fear. When court intrigue led to the execution of her lovers, and when Wu proved unable to save her favorites, she appeared vulnerable, tumbled from her position, and then died.

Was Mohammed sincere? The Koran reads like a sincere document—Muslims believe it to be the spoken words of a single man over the course of a twenty-three-year period between 610 and 633. The Koran rambles, disconnects, contradicts, and radiates vagueness. Vagueness, sometimes called "mystery" makes a religion successful. Vagueness allows for the interpretive skills of scholars to be employed.

This is the real point of religious doctrine, and to attack any single religious teaching as insincere is to miss the point. Christianity was not created by Jesus, and Islam was not created by Mohammed; both came from the inventive minds of later storytellers and scholars and then from any elites who evolved power based on the narratives that had been perpetuated in society.

As elites found their authority based on the narrative, the narrative evolved fundamentalist importance.

This being said, the Islamic holy canon, consisting of the Koran, the *Hadith* (a collection of orally transmitted stories that supposedly explain the time of the Prophet), and the *Sira* (the biography of Mohammed), contains a spurious story involving Mohammed's insincerity. Mohammed's revelations seized him first in the year 610, but his teachings found only rocky ground in his home city of Mecca.

The Umayyad clan that controlled Mecca drove Mohammed away, and he came, by the year 622, to govern a neighboring town of Medina. During the context of war between Medina and Mecca, Mohammed briefly abandoned monotheism and declared that the revelations he had received from Allah via the angel Gabriel allowed for the worship of three traditional Meccan goddesses. This revelation so clearly violated the "there is no god but Allah" declaration that forms the core of Islamic faith that Mohammed's followers neared revolt.

Luckily, Mohammed determined that Satan had hacked his connection with Allah, and that the revelations about the goddesses came not from God but from devil. These "Satanic Verses" got stricken from the record, but the incident remains an embarrassing part of Islamic lore. (The history of Salman Rushdie and his novel with the title of *Satanic Verses* [1988] will not be recounted here, but even a casual observer of the news will be familiar with the impact his book had on the culture of free speech.)

Islam contains no story of death and resurrection, and no core theology about how what constitutes a moral life in this world will equal an eternal reward in the next complicates Islamic theology. Conquer, establish dominance, ring out the call to prayer, collect taxes, allow converts into the Ummah, and repeat; this was Islam's straightforward creed. The Koranic version of Christian scripture features an imposter being crucified in the place of Jesus; Muslims could not conceive of a god who lost to real world power.

Most Muslims practice their religion with only a small amount of devotion, usually by recognizing the high holidays as a means of getting together with family. The most devout Islamic nations tend to have the highest Internet usage; time between prayers gets spent maximizing the loophole that the Koran says nothing prohibiting Wi-Fi. Young people in many of the disabled societies of the Middle East plug into video games as a way of dulling the boredom and avoiding the bombs. Sad, but not insincere.

The Aztecs and Incas of pre-Columbian American civilizations both practiced the art of authoritarian insincerity. The Aztecs conquered neighboring tribes and established a loose empire in a region that roughly corresponds with today's southern Mexico. The Aztecs forced heavy taxation on the surrounding tribes, but the taxes might have been too burdensome for anyone to really pay all the time.

This revealed the real purpose behind the Aztec tribute empire, which was to force outlying tribes into a position where they could not meet the Aztec demands. This provided justification for the Aztecs to storm into their subordinates' villages and conk people on the noggin. The Aztecs carried no piercing weapons, only blunt, because their intent was to incapacitate, not to kill. They would then drag the subordinate back to the capital city of Tenochtitlan.

What stands at the city center usually reveals a good deal about what the people of that civilization value. A typical city in the United States might contain a city center with a public library, a court, and a city council building. This would symbolize that Americans respect free access to information, justice, and democracy. At the center of Tenochtitlan stood a tall set of stone stairs with a sacrificial altar at the top. Their victims, those who failed to pay taxes, got thrown upon the altar where a shaman, with a knife made from carved obsidian, cut the heart out of his sacrifice.

Some part of this system had to be insincere. Either the Aztecs really wanted to terrorize their subordinates into paying taxes and invented a bloodthirsty deity to justify this terror, or else they really did believe in the bloodthirsty gods and imposed taxes so heavy that no one can pay them all of the time, which set up an economic justification for seizing victims.

The Incas of modern-day Peru mummified dead royalty and paraded them through the villages periodically so that the subordinates could have a gander at the corpses of dead leaders. This supposedly contained some kind of religious significance, as the Inca kings claimed to be descended from some otherworldly deity (a common theme in early world civilizations). Reverence for dead political figures may be one of the least sincere of public expressions.

Monuments to the dead, many of them ruinously expensive, can be found across ancient civilizations. It stretches credibility that an Egyptian pyramid, for example, really existed only to keep the rain off a dead pharaoh. The pyramid stood as a symbol that reminded the rubes that the current ruler could claim relation to the withered old bones that lay somewhere on the bottom floor of all that stone. Any ruler who can command the labor and capital necessary for building a structure that honors his deceased predecessor reinforces his own authority in the process.

By holding up the mummified remains of previous rulers, the current Inca king reminded everyone of his own royal lineage and, therefore, of his authority. It would send several messages to the subordinates, the first of them being "you are here because I ordered it," and the implied "you are crying for my grandfather but I am not crying for yours."

The only modern correlation to this can be found in North Korea. If Internet videos not featuring cats are still around by the time you read this, it might be fun to look up what a bout of political mourning looks like in North

Korea. When the body of one of the deceased North Korean dictators is put on parade (two bodies so far, but the chubby and psychopathic eighth-grader who currently runs things looks like he might just be a couple of muffins away from cardiac arrest), subordinates flank the streets and compete to be as demonstratively broken up as possible. Why all the wailing? Sadness for the dead leader equals loyalty to the current one.

Feigned retreats and resignations, though risky, also show the power of insincerity. In the late twelfth century, a Mongol child named Temujin rose from poverty on the steppes above China to unite the warring Mongol tribes under his leadership. The tribesmen bestowed the title of Genghis Khan on Temujin and prepared to conquer the surrounding lands.

The Mongols under Genghis Khan invented psychological warfare and embraced insincerity as a military tactic. The feigned retreat, where the Mongols pretended to gallop away from enemies, gained a series of victories from overconfident foes during the time of Genghis Khan and continued to be a tactic after his death.

In the middle of the thirteenth century, just a few decades after the death of Genghis, a Mongol horde attacked Russia. The Russian knights and nobles, fighting from their heavily muscled steeds, chased the retreating Mongols. The Mongol horsemen rode small horses, almost the size of ponies, that they had bred for endurance. By the time the Mongols "retreated" to flat ground of their choosing, the large Russian war-chargers sagged with exhaustion and the Russian warriors felt the sting of Mongolian arrows.

Insincere retreats require the greatest amount of confidence from an authority figure because the process turns power over to subordinates, even if only temporarily. In the case of the Mongol feigned retreats, the military leadership needed to be confident that they could "run away" from an enemy without this affecting how subordinates viewed their leadership. No one's authority is absolute during a retreat, and it must be harder to cajole an organization into engaging in a ruse than it is an individual.

Soldiers can be executed for retreating during an invasion, but what if a soldier invades during a retreat? That particular problem might take care of itself in the context of war, but the commander of such tactics must be confident that his subordinates will return power to him at the right time. If they do, then his authority can be described as complete.

From Russia comes an example of the most insidious act of authoritative insincerity, which is the feigned resignation. Ivan IV, also called Ivan Grozny, the suffix meaning "Terrible" or "awe inspiring" at once, got sick of the Russian nobility. Ivan had a bad run in the 1560s, losing wars and dealing with unsuccessful domestic policies. Someone probably poisoned his beloved wife, and Ivan's psychological state, which trended toward psychopathy anyway, deteriorated. Apparently, he got sick of the grumbling coming from the boyars, and in December 1564, he quit.

Russian Orthodox Christianity upheld, rather than challenged, the political authority of the czar (a Slavic corruption of the name *Caesar* just as the word *Kaiser* is a German corruption of the word) received his powers directly from a heavily bearded god. To whom, exactly, should Ivan Grozny submit his resignation? It was not clear that a czar could abdicate. Russia's boyar clans, steeped in ancient traditions, did not possess a reputation for creative governmental thinking.

In their defense, no place in the world would develop any kind of representative government for well over a century, not until England's "Glorious Revolution" of 1688, and even that only created a parliamentary monarchy, so for the Russian aristocratic class to imagine a new type of government absent a czar would be a thought too far.

Still, the feigned resignation might be thought of as a single-throw gamble. The czar threw the dice into the hands of his subordinates, and he could only hope for a while that they would throw it back. What if the boyars kept the dice? Ivan Grozny must have known they would not. If and when they did throw the dice back to him, they would do so with the understanding that they had made him complete master of the game. The boyars tossed the dice back and agreed to Ivan's conditions for return.

Ivan merely insisted on total power, and realizing that all authority ultimately rests upon violence, he created his own police force called the *oprichniki*. History records numerous incidents where rulers, leery of those around them, created their own secret police force for protection and power. In a similar way, the Roman emperors after Augustus protected themselves with the Praetorian Guard.

During the Abbasid Dynasty, the sons of the caliph raised private armies to fight it out with their brothers whenever it came time to decide the succession. In this case, the guardsmen came from the outer-lands, which made it easier for their lord to keep them separated from the influence of palace instigators and nobles with designs to take over the throne. In both the Roman Empire and the Abbasid Dynasty, the mercenaries all eventually came to the same conclusion and finally looked at the political authorities and said, "We have the big biceps and the axes, why are we taking orders from you?" Pretty soon, the guardsmen ran things. Only in Russia could the czar keep control of his forces.

Ivan's *oprichniki*, dressed all in black and wearing an insignia of a dustpan and broom, swept up anyone accused of disloyalty to the czar. Thoughts of insurrection never seem to have troubled them. The summer sun sets late in Moscow, and the *oprichniki* made public use of the extended daylight to torture and kill Ivan's opponents. Ivan Grozny's insincere resignation gave him the power he needed to express the full sincerity of his psychopathic impulses onto the Russian people.

If ever there were an Ivan Grozny of the hardwood, it would be former Indiana University basketball coach Bobby Knight. In 1986's *A Season on the Brink: A Year with Bob Knight and the Indiana Hoosiers*, John Feinstein records that Knight used the old insincere resignation trick on his basketball team:

> Knight finally stalked out of the room after asking Alford [the star player], "Will you ever, just once, take charge?" He was back ten seconds later. "You guys sit here for a while and if you still want to have a team, then you come and tell us."
>
> These were the days the players hated most. These were the times that had caused earlier generations to refer to Assembly Hall as "Monroe County Jail." That was what it felt like. The locker room was the cell and the building was the prison. There was no escape. They sat looking at each other. What was there to say? It had all been said. But they had to play the coach's game. So [the players] walked to the coaches' locker room to tell Knight that, yes, they still wanted to have a team. One wonders what would happen someday if the captains walked in and told Knight, "You're right, coach, it's hopeless, let's cancel the season." (1986, 162)

Of course, that would not happen. Only someone in a complete position of authority, where the subordinates rely upon his presence, should ever attempt the insincere resignation. The boyars presumably needed a god-ordained czar for their positions of authority to mean anything. Knight's basketball players could not very well play a game or keep their scholarships or local fame without him. "Let's cancel the season," would not be an option at all. The dice that Knight threw to his players contained invisible strings.

Likewise, Ivan Grozny realized that Russian historical circumstances made it impossible for the boyars to keep their authority without him. Russia covers an expansive territory, one that stretches into the wild east and incorporates people who speak in languages that lack for vowels while worshiping a variety of gods.

The only ways to keep such disparate people together under the banner of a single flag are either to (a) embrace multiculturalism or (b) use military terror. Russia could only exercise the second option, and so Ivan's insincere resignation was not much more of a gamble than Bobby Knight's offer to end the season if his team requested it.

What reveals the insincere resignation to be the province of total authority is that if a subordinate or and equal tries the technique, then the result can only be disastrous. You might think your employer relies upon your skills so much that an insincere resignation will force the bosses to beg you to stay; however, in reality, you have only the smallest of stakes to gamble with, and this does not involve your skills.

You are valuable to a company or organization only to the extent that having to replace you is a hassle. More will be said about this later, but the purpose of mentioning it here is to show that an employee who says, "fine, I quit," in hopes of manipulating a superordinate or the husband who says "I want a divorce" to his wife in hopes of manipulating his way into a greater position of authority both commit a serious error.

Niccolo Machiavelli's advice on insincerity included the specifics of how to exercise power. He offered no philosophical sustenance to subordinates and advisors; having been an unsuccessful subordinate himself, he may not have felt qualified to give advice on that topic. He had time to write *The Prince*, after all, only because he'd been ousted from power after choosing the wrong side in one of Italy's internal political disputes.

Instead, Machiavelli's advice on insincerity included the specifics of how to exercise power. Machiavelli is one of those philosophers whose work does not lend itself well to textbook sidebars and Wiki pages, so the short version of "the ends justifies the means" that gets conveyed to casual philosophers fails to explain the context of his work. Machiavelli sought to fix a disjunction in Western civilization that had to do with the difference between Christian teaching and the actual demands that come from exercising political power.

However one reads the Gospels, and umpteen-hundred different variations of interpretations exist, one can hardly make the case that they can be seen as a handbook for how to gain and keep political power. The Roman authorities crucify Jesus at the end, and the message of Christianity involves the idea that one must live in this world by exercising principles that run counter to what the acquisition of worldly power would require. Christianity teaches that this lifestyle, sustained by faith, will lead to rewards after death when the rules change.

The Christian lives life with the understanding that the principles that guide her actions and decisions will *not* lead her to exercise real-world power. This political and religious misalignment began in the early fourth century; Constantine (274–337) claimed to see a Chi-Rho symbol (Greek cross) hanging in the sky just before he defeated his brother-in-law Maxentius at the Battle of Milvian Bridge. Maxentius drowned in the river, and Constantine's soldiers hacked his head off, stuck it on a pike, and marched into Rome.

Constantine, or his later hagiographers, claimed that the Latin phrase *In Hoc Signo Vinces* shone just underneath the Chi-Rho symbol. The Almighty apparently sent his symbols in Greek but his messages in Latin; translated into English the phrase means "In This Sign, Conquer." Less than insincere, this must surely be an outright lie. Nonetheless, the creation of this myth indicates that Constantine knew little about the nuances of the Christian faith. He seems to have been interested in developing what some historians call Caesaropapism, or the concept of "One God, One Emperor."

The disjunction between polytheism and centralized rule vexed emperors since the time of the Egyptians, with at least one pharaoh, who came to be called Akenhaten (died ca. 1336 BC), tried to put the polytheist priests out of work by killing off their gods and declaring the sun to be the only true lord. Several centuries later, Constantine sought to realign Roman culture by ending polytheism and instituting monotheism.

Never a Christian (few believe tales of his death bed conversion), Constantine probably knew little about the message of Jesus. It's hard to see how he could have. No Bible yet existed, and at least two dozen different handwritten variations of the gospel story made the rounds between groups of believers.

As time went on and the four Synoptic Gospels, meaning "see together" in Greek, made the rounds, a story of Jesus's life congealed and a rough concept of theology developed. The problem, for a Christian emperor, came when the ruler proclaimed to be a Christian but then, through inevitable circumstance, had to burn down a village or two and hang some rebel leaders. This behavior could not be described as forgiving and Christ-like.

The problem in the Western power structure manifested itself just a few decades after the death of Constantine in 334. In 390, Emperor Theodosius ordered his troops to massacre a mob in Thessalonica. Theodosius professed to be a Christian emperor, and either conscience or common sense nagged at him after he gave his instruction because he rescinded his order soon after.

The emperor's troops learned of the retraction only after chopping and spearing about seven thousand people. All this could be considered a good day's work for an ordinary barbarian emperor, but when Theodosius later tried to enter into church, he encountered Bishop Ambrose (now sainted) who refused to let the emperor in until he completed a penance. This posed a fascinating question in Western civilization all the way up until Machiavelli, that question being "who's in charge here?" Or, rephrased, what was more important for a Christian emperor—to act like a Christian or like an emperor?

Hypocrisy, not insincerity, forms in the gap between Christian teaching and the exercise of political power. Hypocrisy, the act of saying one thing and doing another, inspires hatred in subordinates. Fear trumps hatred, but not all princes realize this. Machiavelli wrote that princes should simply abandon Christianity and, with it, hypocrisy. Don't tell the masses that you love them and will forgive and then burn their villages down and hang the rebel leaders when they revolt. This is hypocritical. Tell the masses that if they revolt you will burn their villages down and hang the rebel leaders. That way there is no surprise when it happens. Power should always act with sincere violence.

Machiavelli inspired a new philosophy, described later by Friedrich Nietzsche as anti-Christian, in the sense that this philosophy abandoned meekness and celebrated power. Schopenhaur substituted the "will" to power for forgiveness, and Nietzsche invented a hypothetical *"ubermensch"* or "superman" who embraces the philosophy of power and wields the tools of manipulation with a religious fervency, to directly counter the example of the hypothetical *undermensch* represented by Jesus.

This philosophy of power did eventually manifest itself in twentieth-century politics. Never democratically elected to anything, Adolf Hitler came to power in Germany mostly through luck by the year 1933. Attempts to define Nazism always fall short because the ideology combines a series of hard-to-comprehend ideas. These include *völkisch* back-to-the-soil romanticism, pseudoscientific racism, pseudohistorical notions of history as a race war, and the raw emotional conceit that the German military lost World War I not because of any foreign army but because of a Jewish/Communist stab in the back on the home front. This all congealed around the idea of political power expressed through the will, the party, and ultimately the Führer.

No definition of Nazism will satisfy every aspect of the ideology, but it might be best described simply as institutionalized psychopathy. Trying to make sense of Nazism might be akin to approaching a man with a rosy-stained butchered knife who is surrounded by newly punctured bodies and asking what his motivation was. History suffers no shortage of researchers with a specialty in some aspect of the rise of Nazism, but one day someone should study the rare effect that seeing one's irrational beliefs become true (even for a time) can have on a body politic.

Surely, the early Nazi victories against the forces of democracy must have seemed like evidential assurance for Nazism's core beliefs. Whole regions of the world today remain dominated by political and religious systems that are still living off the memory of centuries-old military victories that once seemed proof of truth. For all of this, Hitler oozed sincerity in his belief systems, so much so that any insincerity in his dealings with other nations seemed justified.

Totalitarian systems of government tend to act sincerely. It is the subordinates in those systems who must act with insincerity, and insincerity from a subordinate position is an art more delicately practiced, but that subject must wait for the next chapter.

We like our insincerity to be fully insincere and evil. In 1939, when the Soviet and Nazi foreign ministers signed the Molotov-Ribbentrop Non-aggression Pact, neither Hitler nor Stalin intended to hold to the principles of the pact as both just used the treaty as an excuse to buy time for a surprise attack on the other. When Hitler ordered an invasion of the Soviet Union on June 22, 1941, he revealed the whole treaty to be the most insincere ever signed by major powers.

It might be worth parsing the statement that "authoritarian systems tend to act sincerely" as this might give pause to anyone steeped in Orwell's *1984* rhetoric. Please remember that Orwell wrote in 1948 and imagined a future scenario where nuclear-armed totalitarian regimes realized that to actually go to war with one another would kill everyone and, thus, spoil all the fun that comes from being in the upper echelon of a totalitarian government.

It's a testament to the effect of Orwell's writing that it should be stated that no scenario as depicted in *1984* ever actually existed in geopolitics. Hitler was sincere in his aims. Stalin was sincere in his. Each employed insincerity not against subordinates, but only as insubordinates or as equals. Insincerity can only be employed when murder and imprisonment are unavailable.

Still, when Orwell's main character, Winston, sees that Eurasia has always been at war with Eastasia, even though he can clearly remember that the two powers had been allied just that morning, it is hard not to think of the ever-changing dictums that generate from any corporate power structure. Eurasia's purpose was never to defeat Eastasia, but to establish a permanent state of war that kept Eurasia's subordinates in their position.

Likewise, when school corporations buy millions of dollars of technology upgrades (with an ever-changing series of thought-destroying doodads) despite reams of research indicating that technology either hurts or provides no gain in student achievement, then one must wonder about the process. Was the point of the technology adoption really to help students, or was the purpose to lock teachers into a constant cycle of being trained by the people in charge? Or, was the point to waste money that might instead be spent on real structural changes that would threaten the position of the people at the top of the hierarchy?

Office workers might express surprise when they find that the corporation's latest technology update actually makes things more difficult than they were before. The purpose, of course, was never to increase efficiency but to ensure that the office managers can force the workers back into the subordinate position of "trainee."

In a totalitarian state, someone who points out the waste of money and time that pointless changes of vision and direction require would be shot or imprisoned. Say the same thing to the person above you in a corporate hierarchy and you know what you will likely hear: "Thanks so much for your feedback."

Historically speaking, authority can enforce insincerity most effectively with direct violence. No slave overseer in the pre–Civil War United States ever had to grin with tobacco-stained teeth and utter the words "thanks so much for your feedback" in response to a slave's complaint. One of the more shocking passages in American literature comes from Frederick Douglass in this description of one of his Maryland overseers:

His savage barbarity was equaled only by the consummate coolness with which he committed the grossest and most savage deeds upon the slaves under his charge. Mr. Gore once undertook to whip one of [the] slaves, by the name of Demby. He had given Demby but a few stripes, when, to get rid of the scourging, he ran and plunged himself into the creek, and was there at the depth of his shoulders, refusing to come out. Mr. Gore told him that he would give him three calls, and that, if he did not come out at the third call, he would shoot him. The first call was given. Demby made no response, but stood his ground. The second and third calls were given with the same result. Mr. Gore then, without consultation or deliberation with any one, not even giving Demby an additional call, raised his musket to his face, taking deadly aim at his standing victim, and in an instant poor Demby was no more. His mangled body sank out of sigh, and blood and brains marked the water where he had stood. (1986 [1845], 66–67)

The appropriately named Mr. Gore justified this destruction of property to his boss by saying that the murder of Demby, while regrettable, prevented the breakdown of discipline that could lead to greater problems later on. The slave master's insincerity came not in the sincere violence used to uphold the system, but in the justifications for slavery. Slaves could not be considered fully human because of their lesser intellect went the justification. Yet, the slave codes declared it illegal to teach a slave to read, something which contradicted the justification for slavery.

Even a barefoot Southern cracker could see the disjunction there; why forbid what should be impossible anyway? Naked violence upheld the system; this was sincere. The stories the slaveholders told themselves provided an insincere set of justifications to assuage guilt and convince the rest of the world of the institution's rightness.

North American slavery, only a small part of the trans-Atlantic system that engulfed Latin America, developed a peculiar racial configuration based on the institution of slavery. In slavery, black- or brown-skinned slaves must act insincerely in order to survive. Slave revolts almost never occurred in the antebellum South because of the overwhelming force of power that the slaveholders held over their breathing property. To the extent that slaves could revolt, they tended to do so by exaggerating their stupidity "I broke another shovel, massa" and finding ways to avoid work.

The nature of the system, however, ensured that slaves who acted insincerely got rewarded by promotion from the fields to the house. Later, during the revolutionary days of the mid-twentieth-century civil rights movement, this provided an analogy for militant factions of the movement. Malcolm X, for example, associated sincerity with rage. Anyone who did not share the rage acted insincerely, and an analogical scale could be associated with this. In slavery, one could act with insincerity and get a job as a house slave, while the more sincere and rebellious labored in the fields.

During the civil rights movement, Harriet Beecher Stowe's character of Uncle Tom became a specific term for any African American person who chose to act happily with the system. In his 1989 autobiography, Malcolm X told Alex Haley about his time in prison after his religious and intellectual awakening:

> I began first telling my black brother inmates about the glorious history of the black man—things they never had dreamed. I told them the horrible slavery-trade truths that they never knew. I would watch their faces when I told them about that, because the white man had completely erased the slaves' past, a Negro in America can never know his true family name, or even what tribe he descended from. . . . I told them that some slaves brought from Africa spoke Arabic, and were Islamic in their religion. A lot of these black convicts still wouldn't believe it unless they could see that a white man had said it. So, often, I would read to these brothers selected passages from white men's books. I'd explain to them that the real truth was known to some white men, the scholars; but there had been a conspiracy down through the generations to keep the truth from black men.
>
> I would keep close watch on how each one reacted. I always had to be careful. I never knew when some brainwashed black imp, some dyed-in-the-wool Uncle Tom, would nod at me and then go running to tell the white man. When one was ripe—and I could tell—then away from the rest, I'd drop it on him, what Mr. Muhammad taught: "The white man is the devil." (1989, 210–11)

Malcolm X noted an age-old problem with trying to start a revolution, one stated by Machiavelli: those in power start with an overwhelming advantage over potential revolutionaries. Anyone wishing to rebel will need allies, and yet every time that a rebel tries to recruit someone, he hands that person a golden ticket. That ticket can be taken to the authorities, and once the rebel gets reported, the person with the ticket can receive a reward from the existing power structure. The reward is more likely than the rebellion.

Revolutionaries, then, must try to make the people they tell about the revolution more afraid of them than they are of the power structure. In the mafia, or in prison, this is accomplished by torturing and killing snitches. In the case of the civil rights movement, militants used peer pressure and the pejorative term *Uncle Tom* to threaten anyone who variated from the militant line.

This concept lives on to an extent in the African American community, and remains one of the more complex internal discussions for black Americans—one that mystifies white people since no equivalent exists in white America. White people do not put on business attire in the morning and have to fear an accusation of betraying a race and movement.

This is one of the great powers of authority—by rewarding insincerity, the power structure creates separate power structures in every corporate entity. When the structure excludes people and rewards others, those who do not receive rewards tend to console themselves with the conceit that anyone who did get reward is a "brownnoser" or "ass-kisser" who only rose in the system due to insincere behavior.

A separate structure then forms where anyone who does not rise in the system gains esteem within that community for the ability to act with sincerity. From management's point of view, these individuals form cadres of resentment based around their inability to rise in the "proper" power structure. From those in the resentment cadre, the power structure becomes something that should be fought and overthrown so that a new structure, one that would reward sincere people like them, could be developed.

Anyone can see the vague justifications for liberal and conservative philosophy in this analysis, as well as shadows of workplace dynamics. This is not to say that either side is right, but merely to frame the perspective on how sincerity and insincerity interplay with one another through human power structures. Individuals who fail to find success in one power structure will create another one where they are esteemed, and individuals inside and outside of each structure tend to see insincerity in each other.

When did the nature of authority in Western civilization begin to embrace the power of insincerity? The short answer is "right after the Protestant Reformation." The Reformation created sincere religious believers who preferred martyrdom to insincerity. The whole thing got bloody and then silly. The era of authoritative insincerity, therefore, came to be with a single phrase, but before revealing what that was, I will add a few words on the historical context.

The French Wars of Religion, where the majority Catholics hacked and shot away at the minority Protestants, called Huguenots for semantic reasons too tedious to delve into here, occurred between 1562 and 1598. In 1589, a Catholic monk hid a knife in the loose sleeve of his robe. He approached the young King Henry III, beckoned him forward as if to whisper to him, then stabbed the king in the gut. Guards hacked the monk into Heaven, and Henry died the next day.

Henry III's death brought Henry IV into power. Henry IV professed to be a Protestant but the Catholics did not like this, and, as previous events showed, the Catholics were in a stabby mood. On July 25, 1593, Henry IV went to the basilica of Saint-Denis and, poof!, became a Catholic. He supposedly told a friend "Paris is worth a mass." This might be apocryphal, but if so, it still perfectly captions the action he took.

Here, for the first time, the mass of subordinates forced authority to act insincerely, and authority found out how much easier this made things. In the 1990s, Saddam Hussein, the "president" of Iraq, used to routinely win elections with 99 percent of the vote. Other global leaders—who dictate rather than preside over legally agreed democratic processes—routinely hold sham elections whose results defy convention.

Why? The insincere election gives the public facade of democracy, and allows certain political figures to act as if they are normalized features of global politics. When George W. Bush and his gang of bungling political theorists decided to cut through Hussein's insincere brand of politics and set up a real democracy, the United States and the world quickly saw just how dangerous sincerity can sometimes be.

Educators might invite students to analyze insincerity's role in any power structure. When authority solicits feedback that is never used to change policy, what does this indicate about authority? In what cases is the role of authority harmful, and if a set of "feedback" guidelines are put in place but do nothing, then why the use of a false front? When is insincerity better than its antonym?

KEY POINTS

- The God of the Old Testament created an insincere scenario by commanding Abraham to sacrifice his son, Isaac, when the real purpose was to test Abraham's faith. Jesus deplored insincere belief, something that defined sincerity in Western culture.
- Historically speaking, direct violence is the most effective way to control the behavior of subordinates. People in authority only use insincerity against subordinates when direct violence is not available.
- Insincerity is to feel one way while acting another while hypocrisy is to say one thing while doing another. The two are not the same. Authority figures who use insincerity do so to create a facade of participation for subordinates.
- Authority figures who can initiate a feigned retreat or insincere resignation tend to have total control because they can temporarily pass authority to subordinates, who then voluntarily give it back.

Chapter Two

Insincerity from the Subordinate

Sarcasm can be defined as insincerity pushed to such an extreme that it becomes noticeable. While sarcasm can be practiced from the superior position, subordinates usually employ it as a means of trying to maintain some control over a situation in which they are relatively powerless. Subordinates tend to employ sarcastic responses only with authority figures who possess relatively little "real" power such as teachers or parents. Parents or teachers must continue parenting and teaching regardless of the ungratefulness of their charges, after all, and so sarcastic responses might trend toward the extreme in both cases.

With *real* authority figures—that is, with people who can actively harm a subordinate or block one's professional progress—the use of sarcasm can be quite dangerous. A boss who detects a trace of sarcasm in an employee's "I'd love to get you some coffee," or who fails to see enough smiling emojis in an e-mail to dissuade any potential of sarcasm, might simply not recommend a subordinate for a pay raise or promotion. The beauty of sarcasm comes from the fact that it presents nothing official for the authority to directly pick up on and punish but, nonetheless, conveys a sense of exasperation from subordinates.

A superior who discounts the power of sarcasm and fails to address the underlying causes of it might find herself in a tough position, however, as the presence of sarcasm indicates (as stated earlier) that the subordinate feels that she has nothing to fear from the authority. The less power that an authority figure possesses, the more sarcasm she will likely have to tolerate from subordinates.

Humorous situations often rely on sarcasm as a central conceit; and an audience's sophistication might be gauged by its ability to pick up on the subtle sarcasm sometimes referred to as "dry wit" or "dry humor." This is the sort practiced by the stereotypical British waiter who must feign a lowered intelligence level in order to serve upper-class twits, but gives the impression of being the only reasonable person in the room.

Less advanced audiences might need to be bashed over the head with sarcastic references; cable television networks, for example, produce thirty-minute snippets of bilge for the pre-and-early-teen crowd that tend to rely almost entirely on exaggerated forms of juvenile sarcasm for their canned laughs. Eleven-year-olds who watch the Disney Channel will be subjected to endless loops of this.

Back in the 1990s, a decade practically dedicated to sarcastic humor, a Canadian comedy troupe called the Kids in the Hall created a sketch around a character who suffered from a speech impediment that made everything he said drip with insincerity. "No wait, I *really* want to be *your* friend," Dave Foley's character implores a potential chum (played by Kevin McDonald) who retreats from the squinting eyes and elongated vowels aimed in his direction. The bit ends with sarcasm-man declaring that he is so lonely. (This sketch is worth finding on YouTube.)

The unfelt apology ranks with sarcasm as a hallmark of subordinate insincerity. "Say it like you mean it," implores the parent to the unruly child when he apologizes to his sister in a sarcastic way. What exactly does it mean to "say it like you mean it?" if, clearly, the apology comes from a fear of punishment?

The authority figure desires sincerity from the subordinate but will settle for an insincere apology sanitized of any trace of sarcasm. The apology may not contain greater sincerity for this, but when the subordinate removes the sarcasm, any trace of rebelliousness against the authority goes with it. The apology, therefore, fails to make peace between the equals but does satisfy the authority figure's desire for control, which was the real point anyway.

History's most famous insincere apology comes from Galileo Galilei, the Italian astronomer who fell afoul of the Catholic Inquisition in the seventeenth century. In that early era of the Scientific Revolution, new types of lenses made their way into Western Europe. Galileo made work of them to create one of those spy-glass type of telescopes often associated with pirates, and, in the first month of the year 1610, he turned his telescope upward at the night sky. Two celestial objects illuminate the darkness above all others in the month of January: the Earth's moon and the gas giant of Jupiter.

Galileo studied both Earth's moon and Jupiter with his new observational tool. Galileo's genius spanned over at least four seemingly disparate fields of knowledge; he obviously could build with the talent of an engineer, employ the mathematics of physics and astrophysics, write with the talent of an essayist, and sketch with the talent of a practiced artist. He recorded his observations, sketched images of the moon with all its crags and through its phases, and wrote up his conclusions with clear explanations and wit.

Authority figures tend not to appreciate talent from subordinates, particularly if that talent seems rarer or more impressive than whatever bureaucratic skills that the superordinate practiced to get into his position. Any subordinate who thinks that talent and impressive work will help him to rise in a hierarchy might like to study any part of history at any time to be disabused of the notion. Galileo could not help himself; he suffered from arrogance and could not suffer fools, and he could claim to be the first human being on the planet to observe certain kinds of celestial phenomena. What's that do for the ego?

When he monitored Jupiter with his new spyglass, three and then four little dots of light appeared next to the planet. Subsequent observations showed that these dots moved around Jupiter, making them moons. What the observational data showed was not as important as the fact that the observational data existed at all.

Galileo could see the moons, night after night, which meant that the sun's light bounced off them continually. If Galileo could see the moons consistently, then this indicated that the sun did not rotate around the Earth, but rather that the sun shone at the center of the rotational system. This confirmed the heliocentric theory previously posited by Polish astronomer Nicolas Copernicus theorized in his 1543 book *De Revolutionibus*.

In 1610, Galileo published his findings in a book called *The Starry Messenger* and then managed to quit his professorial job (in all times, it seems to be the goal of most professors to become so renowned that he or she can eliminate teaching responsibilities altogether) and found refuge in the republican city of Florence, Italy. Protected by a free-thinking duke, Galileo continued his visual explorations of the heavens and felt free to think without the constraints of geocentric theory.

The astronomer grew bolder with every finding; one can only imagine what it feels like to be the first human being in the history of the world to see certain phenomena in the dark infinity of space. Galileo looked at the same thing that everyone else had, but did so with a more powerful eye, and this revealed that previous theories regarding the heavens and the human place in them had been based on a limited knowledge of the universe. In 1613, he published a book on sunspots and wrote, in clear language, in favor of the Copernican system.

Catholicism never squashed ideas to the extent that lay historians sometimes assume. Throughout the medieval period, the only place where a literate person could find intellectual conversation would have been in a monastery. The church nurtured ideas among the elites in the doctoral program (the term *doctor* being Latin for "teacher") and tolerated all sorts of discussion as long as the juicy bits that might make someone question the veracity of the whole enterprise never actually got to the masses.

At first, the Catholic authorities blessed Galileo's evidential findings but officially disagreed with the theory he employed to describe the evidence. In these early days of the Scientific Revolution, the relationship between theory and evidence had yet to develop into the modern conception. No one persecuted the astronomer, but in the year 1616, a theological council decreed that Galileo's sun-centered theories should be considered wrong on theoretical grounds.

Afterward, Pope Paul V did warn his subordinate not to press the idea of a "solar" system too hard, but Galileo still suffered no punishment. In 1623, Pope Paul V died, and a cardinal (Latin for "important person") became the new pontiff and donned the name of Urban VIII. Galileo considered the new pope a friend, and in their discussions with one another, the pope apparently thought he made it clear to the astronomer that he could publish anything that he wanted as long as the ideas continued to be labeled as hypothetical.

For the next half dozen years, Galileo busied himself writing a book that he titled *Dialogue Concerning the Two Chief World Systems*, a somewhat fictionalized account of three men discussing whether the planetary system was geocentric or heliocentric. He named the defender of the earth-centered system *Simplicio*, meaning "simpleton," and Simplicio sounded suspiciously like the pope.

No one can be more miserable than a hyperintelligent subordinate, so we can imagine Galileo's frustrations as his intellectual inferiors but political superiors tried to restrict his genius. It had been Galileo, not Urban VIII, who had caught God's favor and first seen the celestial wonders of deep space. Did Galileo consider this a mandate from God that he, and not the pope, was in charge?

If so, Galileo forgot who wielded the actual tools of power, and that all power rests in some way upon the ownership of violence. Rome issued a summons to Galileo. Galileo said he was too sick to attend, and the pope offered to have the troublesome natural philosopher delivered forcibly in chains. At this point, Galileo felt well enough that he decided he could probably make the trip on his own.

In 1633, Galileo recanted his position, no doubt through gritted teeth, by stating the most insincere apology in Western civilization's history. Except for the threat of violence inherent in the process, the event would seem almost comic, as if the Catholic authorities could intimidate an ailing old man and somehow make the planetary rotations obey their dogmas. Galileo must have understood the torture that awaited him should he defy his betters and, therefore exercised a little good sense and signed a lengthy document recanting all he had thought, said, and published.

Having done all this, legend has it that he muttered *Eppur si muove*, which is Latin for "But it does move," in reference to the Earth. Even passive fans of the history and philosophy of science know this story well, but the purpose of recounting it here is to mark the incident's important place in the history of insincerity. By issuing a false apology, Galileo ended an era of religious sincerity and brought in a new era of scientific and philosophical insincerity.

Galileo's insincerity must be contrasted with Martin Luther's blatant sincerity. In 1517, Luther hammered his 95 theses to the door of a church in Wittenberg, Germany, and inaugurated the Protestant Reformation. The operative part of the word *Protestant*, "protest," indicated Luther's opinion toward authority. Psychoanalyzing historical figures may be one of the more spurious activities that a writer can engage in, but with that caveat stated, few would disagree that Luther tended to have both antiauthoritarian and authoritarian personality characteristics.

In 1521, when Luther found himself called on the carpet before Western Europe's big shots at the Diet of Worms, he stated his intentions immediately by layering on the sarcasm. When asked if he wished to recant, Luther began with:

> *Most Serene Lord Emperor, Most Illustrious Princes, Most Gracious Lords . . . I beseech you to grant a gracious hearing to my plea, which, I trust, will be a plea of justice and truth; and if through my inexperience I neglect to give to any their proper titles or in any way offend against the etiquette of the court in my manners or behavior, be kind enough to forgive me, I beg, since I am a man who has spent his life not in courts but in the cells of a monastery; a man who can say of himself only this, that to this day I have thought and written in simplicity of heart, solely with a view to the glory of God and the pure instruction of Christ's faithful people.* (Harvard Rhetorical Society, http://www.hcs.harvard.edu/~rhetoric/luther.htm)

If an Insincerity Museum ever gets built, this excerpt will be the first thing displayed. Again, sarcasm may only be employed by subordinates who fear nothing from the superordinate. All power derives from the fact that one party wants something from the other. If you want a promotion or an award from a superordinate, that endows the hierarchy with power.

In some cases, the hierarchy can create conditions where the subordinate merely wants the pain of torture to stop or wants to gain a lightened sentence of some kind. If the subordinate can train himself to not care what the authorities do to him, then a kind of mental freedom can be attained.

Luther goes on to assure the authorities that he will recant his teachings only if it can be proven, through scripture, that his work contains errors. He accepts the authority of scripture but not the authority of the Catholic authorities and his eventual refusal to take back anything that he said. His refusal, therefore, to speak insincerely broke Christendom forever.

As has already been established, Jesus considered sincerity to be a virtue. Sincere believers prayed in private and carried faith with them in a matter that could only be seen by the Almighty through the heart but could be demonstrated to the public through quiet actions. Sincere belief in Catholic doctrines seemed important to the authorities. When political expediency made it possible to hurl the condemnation of insincere belief at a vulnerable population, then insincerity itself evolved into a crime.

In order to understand Luther in 1521, one must go back to the year 1415, at a time when the Catholic hierarchs proclaimed no less than three men to be the true pope. The cardinals could no longer keep the public from seeing the political machinations behind the Holy See. This may have contributed to a larger problem of the breakdown of authority that began when the church itself proved incapable of stopping the Black Plague and its viral aftershocks in the fourteenth century.

Whatever the case, subordinates across Europe suddenly found themselves feeling less subordinate than before. Peasants revolted in England, and a pair of Christian theologians, one English and the other Czech, challenged the authority of the church.

The Englishman John Wycliff taught that the Bible should be accessible to ordinary believers, and this meant translating the text into English. The Czech theologian Jan Hus preached a sincere message about the danger of religious hierarchy to his followers. Both Wycliff and Hus thought and taught that the church power players seemed more interested in worldly wealth and power than in saving souls. Sincere religious belief needed no help from hierarchs, and ordinary Christians could read and interpret the Bible for themselves if given access.

The English Channel later saved England from Napoleon and Hitler, and it probably also protected Wycliff from the Roman authorities. Hus lived in the center of Europe, and this magnified the danger of his words. In 1415, when the church authorities decided that the three-pope problem harmed the ability to control Europe, they called the Council of Constance. It must have seemed prudent to solve all their problems in one place and at the same time, so they invited Jan Hus to attend and promised him safe passage.

The promise was insincere. The authorities seized Hus upon his arrival, tied him up, and burned him alive. The church did whittle itself down to one pope, but Hus's death and the tricky way in which he had been insincerely invited to his own death overshadowed any positive accomplishment. The murder enraged his followers. They rebelled and drove out the mother church.

For Catholic hierarchs, this incident of heretic burning led to a loss of territory in Hus's home region. The Council of Constance is generally considered to be the last major event of the medieval period; how appropriate that the light at the end of the long historical tunnel known as the Dark Ages turned out to be the burning corpse of a heretic. How significant that the smoke from Hus's body still hovered over Europe over a century later; because of Hus, the church authorities could not burn Luther.

In the time between Hus and Luther, Catholic hard-liners, perhaps threatened by the lessening of control that could be seen and sensed across Europe, conjured up the Inquisition. The Inquisitors targeted insincerity more than heresy, and converted Iberian Jews, called *conversos*, suffered the most because the authorities suddenly worried that their conversions had come from expediency rather than from the heart. Better to be rid of them, came the eventual decision in 1492's Expulsion, and rescue their land and wealth into the safe harbor of Ferdinand and Isabella's treasury.

It all got too insincere with the excessive selling of forgiveness. The printing press opened the bottleneck between new ideas, religious and societal frustration, and the general public. When he wrote his 95 Theses, Luther, a man of the monkish cells, knew little of the printing press, and some unknown person took the Theses from the door in Wittenberg and placed it on a press.

Suddenly notorious, Luther quickly learned how to write for the new medium, and he combined a genius for theology with the curse words of a farmer. He employed the sarcastic rage of a man whose sincere faith and talents now turned themselves against the very authorities that had once nurtured him.

An age of religious sincerity dawned across Europe, and the word *catholic* (meaning "universal") morphed from a lowercase ordinary adjective to an uppercase positive noun. The Catholic Church would be one among many. Then religion became political, as nobles across Europe realized that, by converting to one of the protest sects, they became free to seize any church lands within their domains.

Henry VIII of England converted his lands from Catholic to Anglican, whatever that means, by adopting the protestant ethos of the biblical translator (from Latin to English in this case) William Tyndale. That particular conversion story, affected because of Henry's desire for a divorce from his aging Spanish wife and former sister-in-law, is so well known that to repeat the story here would be tedious. Yet the English circumstances at the time provided the right conditions for sincere belief to show itself.

Thomas More, the author of *Utopia*, a book that smacks of insincerity, by the way, since More seemed intent on avoiding any criticism of actual society by placing his perfect society in a mythological "nowhere" state and chose the language of fiction and fantasy rather than developing an actual plan for societal reform. Anyway, More stood up for the interests of the mother church and bravely died on her behalf, an act for which he later received sainthood.

Walking to one's death on behalf of an ideal may be considered the ultimate act of sincerity in the same way that condemnation of someone to death amounts to the ultimate expression of political power. Soon enough, the political and religious labels got switched in England. Henry's daughter through his first wife Catherine was the unlovely Mary Tudor. Since Mary practiced an ardent Catholicism, the royal bureaucrats attempted to pull a shenanigan by making a girl named Lady Jane Grey, queen.

Mary thought not. Lady Jane Grey is now known as the "nine days queen," which indicates just how well things went for her. Mary and her allies marched on London and took power through direct means.

Now queen, Mary Tudor, Catholic, ticked off, and intent to rip the pages of Protestantism from the English history books, ordered the deaths by burning of over four hundred Anglicans during her time. She earned the moniker of "Bloody Mary," and like many a dictator, royal or not, she practiced a direct form of power. Nothing about Bloody Mary could be described as insincere. She wanted to see heretics burn, so burn they did.

Many of her victims reveled in the persecutions; all of these were opportunities to show Jesus their sincere belief! Sincerity and stoicism had never been so much on display, even as the crowds took in the sound of screams and endured the smell of sizzling human fat.

John Foxe chronicled all this in his *Book of Martyrs*, which could be considered the classical work on the topic of religious sincerity. The martyrs competed for the finest deaths, convinced, one assumes, that such an act proved the sincerity of their belief. This brings up the great paradox of sincerity.

A high level of sincerity, particularly in moral matters, tends to give an individual a bump in the esteem of her peers. Unfortunately, by demonstrating such sincere belief, the individual dies before she can receive any accolades. Most people would probably prefer to get credit for having the willingness to die for a belief more than they would actually like to die for a belief.

Who among us would not like to be at work, or among family, and then be presented with the opportunity to jump on a grenade that some shadowy terrorist suddenly rolls into the scene only to realize, after a few moments of anxious sprawling, that the grenade was a dud? Oh, the accolades one would receive! "You were willing to die for us!" everyone would say. Queue the ticker tape and chocolate milkshakes. In this scenario, one would get a raise in status without actually being splattered upon the walls.

Of course, one can presume that Foxe's martyrs believed something close to this very thing; they would suffer the flames for a short while and then enter into paradise where the act of walking through fire would only enhance their status. Their charred flesh left in the ashes, the martyrs would seek a reward from Jesus in a different kind of glow.

To call *The Book of Martyrs* as it appeared in 1563 a "book" would be to misunderstand the intent of the work. The book included sixty woodcuts and weighed several pounds. It was something meant to have physical and figurative weight and to take a central place on a desk or podium. In the flickers of candlelight, the reader could be inspired by the horrors of the bonfire.

Was the story of Jesus the real inspiration for sincere martyrdom? Jesus himself fits well into a Western tradition where death tested sincerity, and one's ability to suffer inflictions of pain and torture prior to death only increased the level of sincerity. Plato, in his dialogue *Phaedo* tells us that Socrates, too, died well.

Socrates told jokes and uttered misogynistic comments right up to the end, but Socrates died as an old man and Jesus, supposedly, not really at all. Jesus believed he would live forever and reign as a king in the afterlife while Socrates anticipated that the Hemlock he swallowed would produce only a few moments of discomfort before the end.

Likewise is true for the 298 Spartans that Herodotus carved out of imaginary muscle, all of whom fell before the Persian horde of King Xerxes, or perhaps they all drowned in their own testosterone. Led by King Leonidas and awash in adrenaline, the Spartans probably barely felt the spears and arrows of their enemies. Death in the maelstrom, one assumes, comes lightly felt.

The Greek tradition of the sincere Stoic infuses the New Testament narratives of Jesus, and provides the cultural framework for understanding Foxe's martyrs. The Stoic showed no hysterical emotion because she commanded herself so completely that no punishment from authority could create any harm. True freedom came from a personal cultivation of inward morals until acting insincerely became an impossibility.

Given that sincerity can be measured, usually in hindsight, by one's willingness to suffer and die for an ideal or a person, Western literature's most sincere figure is not Socrates, Jesus, or Leonidas but a teenaged girl named Antigone. Antigone comes from the imagination of the Athenian playwright Sophocles (496–406 BC) just as surely as Socrates was conjured up by Plato, Leonidas by Herodotus, or Jesus from a host of anonymous authors.

The play *Antigone* concludes a trilogy known as *The Three Theban* plays. Antigone's brother perished on a battlefield while fighting against the forces of a tyrant named Creon for the control of the Thebes. Creon, victorious, decreed that the man's body should rot on the field and be a public disgrace to his name. Antigone's sister, Ismene, knows of Antigone's defiant wish to bury her brother but refuses to help her sister dig the hole. By creating the character of the sister, Sophocles develops the heroism of Antigone through her opposite reflection in the same way that Plato created a host of students who try to dissuade their teacher from killing himself.

Sophocles combines the emotions of a teenager with just enough eloquence to make the play's dialogue both believable and clear. Antigone begins her conversation with King Creon as an archetype of Stoic defiance.

Creon, indeed, seems to signal that he would accept an insincere apology, perhaps by allowing Antigone to plead ignorance to the laws:

> **Creon:** You, you bending your head to the ground, do you confess or do you deny having done this?
>
> **Antigone:** I both confess I did it, and I do not deny that I did not.
>
> **Creon:** You may take yourself where you please, freed from the heavy charge. But do you tell me not at length, but briefly, did you know the proclamation forbidding this?
>
> **Antigone:** I knew it. And why should I not? It was plain.
>
> (Sophocles 1982, 81)

Antigone, intent on keeping her sincerity, goes on to insult Creon by stating that she knew of his law, but since it emanated from an illegitimate authority (Creon himself) rather than from the gods, she felt no compulsion to follow it. Given a chance to issue an insincere apology and save herself, Antigone instead issues a sincere belief and decides to suffer what comes.

Creon's wicked intellect conceives of the worst kind of death for both a literary martyr and an adolescent girl. Antigone will not sip death from a flagon or feel the piercing of nails in her hands and feet—nothing flashy before the crowds. No arrows will blot out the sun on their way to deliver her a death in the fog of battle. She will walk alone into the quiet dark of a standing tomb. As a literary device, the thought of entombment should give pause to any reader or audience member, and cause a reflection on the whole concept of sincere courage. That poor girl, at an age when the comfort of friends seems more important than anything else, left to die from the darkness.

Sophocles, having imagined this cold horror, drops the archetypal robes from his character and reveals her to be just a frightened young lady:

> **Antigone:** O tomb! O bridal chamber! O excavated, ever-guarded dwelling! Where I got to mine own, of whom now perished prosperine has received the greatest number among the dead and of whom I descend the last, and by a fate far more wretched, before having fulfilled my term of life!
>
> (Sophocles 1982, 105)

She goes on like that for a while, wailing as a teenaged girl, who suddenly sees her immediate fate in a darkened cave, will. Fear and sadness seize a character who suddenly becomes just a girl, and stoicism be damned, she weeps for her lost future. Incapable of insincerity, she displays her feelings before her last audience. This passage of the play reveals not only the brilliance of Sophocles but also the problem with sincerity; it can seem a little emo. One wonders if Antigone could maybe curb the emotion a bit and try to run away or something.

In fact, she is so sincere that the play nearly wanders into what the literary critic and science fiction author James Blish (1921–1975) has called an "idiot plot," meaning that the entire dramatic edifice requires that the main character act like an idiot. Antigone walks into her predicament like teenagers in slasher movies walk out into the garage to inspect a strange noise, leaving the audience shouting out better ideas.

And here is what we might say to Antigone: *just let your brother's body rot in the field, girl.* Or bury it and then plead innocence through ignorance. Here is what we may say to the Protestant martyrs: tell the Catholic powers that you believe in the powers of the saints, whatever, it's not worth getting tortured over, particularly if no religious figure exists in the afterlife to offer you a little cake and punch afterward. (Antigone, by the way, does finally show a little good sense by hanging herself before she got shut into the cave, an act that gives her a little credit for intelligence.)

This is where one finds the great divide between the sincere and insincere; the insincere person can't help but wonder if the sincere believer isn't a bit of a sap, someone who cannot critically examine the situation and conclude that you won't actually choke on the apology or the communion wafer, and that insincere bow of the head before the king might actually be preferable, to one's family and friends at least, to the act of walking into the flames or into the tomb. Imagine if Sophocles had allowed for Creon's original death sentence to be carried out. What would *Antigone II*, featuring scene after scene of the main character's slow death in a lightless grave, do for the conceit of sincerity?

Here we return to Galileo, who broke with a Western literary and philosophical tradition and simply said "I'm sorry," even though he was not. A student of the sixteenth and seventeenth century may burst out and cheer upon learning of Galileo's blatant insincerity. *Finally,* in this era where men and women walked proudly to be burned at the stake as a sign of their religious sincerity, someone showed a little bit of good sense. The whole Galileo episode, in fact, created a vast misunderstanding about the concept of insincerity and its relationship with authority.

Nobody got insincerity and its relationship to subordinates and authority more wrong than Orwell. In *1984* (1949), Orwell writes with the conceit that the goal of a totalitarian state is to burn sincere love and belief into the minds of subjects. Until that can be achieved, the state creates permanent surveillance for the purpose of ensuring that subjects exist in a constant state of outward obedience. For a freethinker like the main character, Winston, this means that he must exhibit insincerity at all times. Orwell's fascination with insincere speech permeates his novels and essays, but he misjudged the relationship between insincerity and authority that forms the central plot of *1984*.

In that novel, the state itself, represented by the ever-watching Big Brother, keeps up a constant public facade of insincerity. It does so through an ever-varying set of alliances and wars:

> The Party said that Oceania had never been in alliance with Eurasia. He, Winston Smith, knew that Oceania had been in alliance with Eurasia as short a time as four years ago. But where did that knowledge exist? Only in his own consciousness, which in any case must soon be annihilated. And if all others accepted the lie which the Party imposed—if all records told the same tale—then the lie passed into history and became truth. "Who controls the past," ran the Party slogan, "controls the future: who controls the present controls the past." And yet the past, though of its nature alterable, never had been altered. Whatever was true now was true from everlasting to everlasting. It was quite simple. All that was needed was an unending series of victories over your own memory. "Reality control," they called it; in Newspeak, "doublethink." (Orwell 1990 [1949], 32)

The more control the Party (an archetype for any power structure) the more outwardly insincere it can be. This is because the subordinates fear the authorities to such a great extent that "raising one's hand" to ask a question or point out a logical flaw would invite all sorts of bad recriminations. From the Party's perspective, the goal would not be to create total belief, but to drive the subjects to a point of constant insincerity. *Doublethink* remains in the culture—and stays relevant through its constant usage among media personalities—but another of Orwell's word coinages might actually be more interesting and relevant:

> It was terribly dangerous to let your thoughts wander when you were in any public place or within range of a telescreen. The smallest thing could give you away. A nervous tic, an unconscious look of anxiety, a habit of muttering to yourself—anything that carried with it the suggestion of abnormality, of having something to hid. In any case, to wear an improper expression on your face (to look incredulous when a victory was announced, for example) was itself a punishable offense. There was even a word for it in Newspeak: *facecrime*, it was called. (1990 [1949], 54)

Doublethink and facecrime both enforced insincerity onto the subordinates, and the Party or Big Brother molded both concepts around the idea that subordinates likely believed something different from what they outwardly displayed. For the Party, the problem with facecrime is not so much that the individual fails to really believe the propaganda, but that he dared to publicly show this.

A momentary emotional lapse that results in a show of incredulity at the announcement of a victory, for example, amounts to an outward display of sincerity. Hence, the problem: facecrime is the crime, but doublethink is the advice to subordinates on how to avoid committing the crime. A subordinate must alter his consciousness and change his memories so that a moment of sincerity will not cause him to slip and commit a facecrime.

Once the reader understands this, the central conceit of the novel makes no sense. At the outset of the book, the Party stands already in a position of supreme power. Through a process of constant change and monitoring, the subordinates in the state exist in a perpetual state of insincerity to the point where Winston himself hopes only to reconnect with his "real" inner self just before bedtime, or thinks a sexual dalliance with the woman who turns out to be a honey trap amounts to an act of political defiance.

When he finally encounters O'Brien, the Party member assigned to break him, Winston gets to read the Party's handbook for control, with the pillars of the Party being the Newspeak phrases of Ignorance Is Strength, War Is Peace, and Freedom Is Slavery. From the section War Is Peace, Winston reads:

> In one combination or another, these three superstates [Eurasia, Oceania, and Eastasia] are permanently at war, and have been so for the past twenty-five years. War, however, is no longer the desperate, annihilating struggle that it was in the early decades of the twentieth century. It is a warfare of limited aims between combatants who are unable to destroy one another, have no material cause for fighting, and are not divided by any genuine ideological difference. (Orwell 1990 [1949], 153)

The secret document goes on to state that the powers of the world now each possess weapons of such mass destruction that a real war, rather than the pseudo-wars waged on the far distant frontiers of each region, would destroy the power base of each area. Chess players who cannot defeat each other seek only to keep the game going, not to burn the board. Later, the secret document states:

> The primary aim of modern warfare (in accordance with the principles of doublethink, this aim is simultaneously recognized and not recognized by the directing brains of the Inner Party) is to use up the products of the machine without raising the general standard of living. Ever since the end of the nineteenth century, the problem of what to do with the surplus of consumption goods has been latent in industrial society. (Orwell 1990 [1949], 155)

At this point, it is worth pausing to ask the question, "Why is *1984* considered a great novel?" The main character's major characteristic is his passiveness; he's an archetype of a slightly intelligent individual living in a totalitarian society. The novel's plot involves him getting baited into an Inner Party intrigue, where the bad guys then reveal their plot to him.

The problem with the book is that the Party seems to want sincerity, not insincerity, from its subjects, and this misunderstands the nature of power. The act of making someone who feels one way *act as if* he feels the way you want him to is the expression of power. When someone feels one way and acts the same way, he acts freely and so authority exercises *no* power.

To explain, we might reference the fable most associated with insincerity. This is, of course, *The Emperor Has No Clothes*, by Hans Christian Andersen. The fable's plot is that an emperor hires a tailor without talent. The tailor weaves the emperor a new set of fine clothing out of nothing, and when the emperor emerges from his chamber in the nude and parades through the halls, he seems convinced that he is actually clad in fine new garments.

All the sycophants in the castle pretend to admire the emperor's new clothes even though they can see the tuft of his pubic hair and the dangle of his testes. The emperor, thrilled by the reaction, decides to take the fashion show public and takes an open carriage out into the streets. The throngs of subjects all ooh and aah over this spectacle until one small boy, presumably ignorant of the concept of dungeons, steps forward and laughs at the emperor's nakedness. As he points, everyone ceases with their insincere appreciations, and the emperor suddenly stands naked before them.

Fables tend to possess fairly clear morals to their stories, but the tale of the naked emperor perplexes. Is it about false flattery, and therefore insincerity? The people in the crowds act insincerely, certainly, when first confronted with the naked emperor. When one child refuses to act insincerely, the whole facade comes crashing down, and the emperor stands nude and powerless.

The moral now gets choked in weed-like complexities. The moral of the story might very well be about the power of central authority. It takes a true strongman to walk around naked while everyone under his control pretends to adore his new finery. Standing ovations of ten to fifteen minutes used to greet Joseph Stalin at the end of his speeches back when the Boss controlled the Soviet state using the same tactics he'd learned as a gangland terrorist. Still, one wonders if even he could have stood before the terrified members of his politburo in nothing but his Georgian birthday suit and demanded that they pretend he wore the uniform of the top comrade.

Hitler, his muscles depleted of definition because of his vegetarian diet, always looked squishy, and psychopathic ranting can hardly count as exercise. He never would have sieg heiled anyone in the nude, and was even so concerned that his body might betray him as something other than an *ubermensch* that he drew up specific rules about avoiding any kind of public athletic contests. Would Der Führer still have been able to command legions if they'd seen him saluting in so much as a pair of boxer shorts? Probably not.

We may therefore infer from history that Hans Christian Andersen's naked emperor must have been one bad son of a gun to walk out of the palace bare as the day he first saw daylight and daring anybody in the crowd to point this out. We can picture him, strutting about with his flaccid junk practically daring anyone to stifle a giggle. When everyone who works for you not only refuses to point out your nudity but also pretends to like your clothes, and when the peasants all follow suit the moment you drop the drawbridge and show them the sun and the moon, well, *you have got control of things*.

So the kid who points this out likely didn't know what happened in the corner of a dungeon, and failed to put on a smile and say something admiring about the boss's new pantaloons. He is the fairy tale version of Emmett Till, the kid from a former free state who didn't know that, south of the Mason Dixon line, he was supposed to pretend that a pretty white lady wasn't pretty. Till whistled and got killed by redneck terrorists. What happened to the little boy who pointed out the emperor's nudity?

That's the perplexing part. For the emperor to hold so much power over the people he must have had a reputation for terror. Subordinates in a position of living in terror do not rally together until the power structure looks like it might shift. Expressing sincerity in a totalitarian state can get you tortured and killed. By pointing out the emperor's nudity, the boy catalyzes the crowd, and each laugh layers on the next until the giggles reach a critical mass. Suddenly, as the power looks to shift, it becomes more personally advantageous to join the gigglers than the deniers.

Yet, for the emperor the point of power cannot be to make the crowds genuinely believe he is clothed. This would rob him of authority. His power lies in the very fact that he can stand there bare naked in front of his kingdom and make everyone pretend like they believe the lie. The emperor understands the nature of power better than Big Brother and, ultimately, better than Orwell.

At the end of *1984*, when Winston loves Big Brother, he becomes as free as the Spartans who fought against Xerxes. Each of the Spartans considered themselves to be free individuals whose actions exactly matched their inward feelings; the *agoge* system generated true believers, but it did so for the purpose of defending a lifestyle and culture against real threats. Orwell's Party merely seeks to exercise power over subordinates. To make true believers out of subordinates would be to destroy the power of the Party and create a society of individuals.

The heads of authoritarian societies certainly have not and do not seem to concern themselves very much with whether their subordinates sincerely believe or not. Does Kim Jung Il really care if the tears shed for his father and grandfather come from truly felt emotion? Do the Iranian theocrats care that women in Tehran typically tear off their headscarves the moment they cross the thresholds into their apartments or dorms?

Did Joseph Stalin ever worry that the minutes-long standing ovations that he received after his speeches might not have been heartfelt demonstrations over the beauty of his Communist rhetoric? No, power comes from forcing someone to do something she does not want to do, and subordinates in such situations must decide what an expression of sincerity in such a situation is worth.

To understand insincerity and its relationship to power, one should skip *1984* and read Joseph Heller's *Catch-22*, which is the classic on the topic. The main character, the World War II American bombardier named Yossarian, acts as an insincere subordinate against an insincere authority. Yossarian proves that the subordinate's main response to insincere authority tends to be a cynicism that gets repressed in situations where the subordinate must interact with authority but then gets expressed in situations where the subordinate exercises control.

In fact, an analysis of *Catch-22* would have fit easily in the last chapter about the power of insincerity from the position of authority, but since the book's main character is a subordinate, and since *Catch-22* provides a counter to *1984*, the analysis fits better here. This passage, where Yossarian talks to a psychologist named Doc Daneeka about the potential of getting out of flying any more combat missions, captures authoritative insincerity and deserves to be quoted in full:

Yossarian . . . decided right then and there to go crazy.

"You're wasting your time," Doc Daneeka was forced to tell him.

"Can't you ground someone who's crazy?"

"Oh, sure. I have to. There's a rule saying I have to ground anyone who's crazy."

"Then why don't you ground me? I'm crazy. Ask Clevinger."

"Clevinger? Where *is* Clevinger? You find Clevinger and I'll ask him."

"Then ask any of the others. They'll tell you how crazy I am."

"They're crazy."

"Then why don't you ground them?"

"Because they're crazy, that's why."

"Of course they're crazy," Doc Daneeka replied. "I just told you they're crazy, didn't I? and you can't let crazy people decide whether you're crazy or not, can you?"

Yossarian looked at him soberly and tried another approach. "Is Orr crazy?"

"He sure is," Doc Daneeka said.

"Can you ground him?"

"I sure can. But first he has to ask me to. That's part of the rule."

"Then why doesn't he ask you to?"

"Because he's crazy," Doc Daneeka said. "He has to be crazy to keep flying combat missions after all the close calls he's had. Sure, I can ground Orr. But first he has to ask me to."

"That's all he has to do to be grounded?"

"That's all. Let him ask me."

"And then you can ground him?" Yossarian asked.

"No. Then I can't ground him."

"You mean there's a catch?"

"Sure there's a catch," Doc Daneeka replied. "Catch-22. Anyone who wants to get out of combat duty isn't really crazy."

There was only one catch and that was Catch-22, which specified that a concern for one's own safety in the face of dangers that were real and immediate was the process of a rational mind. Orr was crazy and could be grounded. All he had to do was ask; and as soon as he did, he would no longer be crazy and would have to fly more missions. Orr would be crazy to fly more missions and sane if he didn't, but if he was sane he had to fly them. If he flew them he was crazy and didn't have to; but if he didn't want to he was sane and had to. Yossarian was moved very deeply by the absolute simplicity of his clause of Catch-22 and let out a respectful whistle.

"That's some catch, that Catch-22," he observed. (Heller 2011 [1961], 54–55)

Catch-22 reflects the CYA (Cover Your Ass, if you didn't know) mentality of all corporations because the one argument that a subordinate can make to Human Resources if she gets into trouble is that the bosses "failed to train me on ____" and this means that the facade of training must be kept up, not for the purpose of actually training or educating anyone, but to prevent the subordinate from making an argument for his own defense should he get called into Human Resources for a "talk."

In Yossarian's case, he faces a military protocol that has evolved into the pinnacle of insincerity, and even a cynic like Yossarian can do nothing but show his appreciation for such a marvel of CYA. The thinking, Heller wryly indicates, is that there must be some protocol for removing pilots with mental health issues, but the paradoxical process itself prevents Yossarian or any other pilot from actually being removed from combat duty.

The stated reason for Catch-22 is to remove insane pilots from combat missions, but the unstated purpose was to keep all pilots flying while satisfying a CYA protocol to have something on the books for removing insane pilots.

As Yossarian admired, that's some catch, that Catch-22.

Yossarian responds with a carefully cultivated cynicism, acting insincerely himself every chance he gets by flying away from the action. One of his superiors, Colonel Cathcart, sends his subordinates into dangerous zones just so the bombing patterns will appear more aesthetically pleasing on the photographs. This passage, where Yossarian argues with a patriotic fellow bomber named Clevinger, illustrates subordinate insincerity:

"There are men entrusted with winning the war who are in a much better position than we are to decide what targets have to be bombed."

"We are talking about two different things," Yossarian answered with exaggerated weariness. "You are talking about the relationship of the Air Corps to the infantry, and I am talking about the relationship of me to Colonel Cathcart. You are talking about winning the war, and I am talking about winning the war and keeping alive."

"Exactly," Clevinger snapped smugly. "And which do you think is more important?"

"To whom," Yossarian shot back. "Open your eyes, Clevinger. It doesn't make a damned bit of difference who wins the war to someone who's dead."

Clevinger sat for a moment as though he'd been slapped. "Congratulations!" he exclaimed bitterly, the thinnest milk-white line enclosing his lips tightly in a bloodless, squeezing ring. "I can't think of another attitude that could be depended upon to give greater company to the enemy."

"The enemy," retorted Yossarian with weighted precision, "is anybody who's trying to get you killed, no matter which side he's on, and that includes Colonel Cathcart. And don't you forget that, because the longer you remember it, the longer you might live." (Heller 2011 [1961], 134–35)

Herein lies the problem when authority layers on too much insincerity; the subordinates actually do the work, or, in the case of the military, the fighting. Yossarian complies just enough to keep from getting court-martialed; his goal is to survive the war. To him, sincere belief in a command structure that focuses on the patterns of bombs on a photograph or creates something like a Catch-22 is its own version of insanity.

As can be seen through the examples provided here, sincerity, not insincerity, causes problems for the power structure. True believers point out hypocrisy when it comes from above and then willingly rebel and die for the cause. Insincere believers throw out homage and do what they are told even if they secretly believe elsewhere. Islam, for example, means "submission." Muslims who submit totally to true belief do not always make great subordinates to political authorities. Orwell's novel endures in the public mind more for its gimmicks than its message, but his misunderstanding of the nature of power and its relation to sincerity and insincerity continues to distort public discourse on the topic.

In many power structures, governmental or corporate, subordinates might occupy a position that requires considerably more intelligence than the managerial position requires. In education, for example, teachers and professors must study deeply within a particular subject area, develop meaningful lessons and research, and engage constantly in a dialogue over content and methods with colleagues and students.

This all requires considerably more intelligence than attending meetings, watching students eat lunch, or shaking hands and soliciting funds and public events which is the work of administration. Somehow, however, many a superordinate individual operates under the notion that because she is the "boss" she must be the smartest person in the room. She, of course, may not be smart enough to see that her job does not require the application of great intellect.

The same may be true in American politics. An elected official requires a team of advisors to help him make decisions. Those advisors must read books, earn doctorates, and attend conferences regarding their subject matter.

The politician must simply become elected, and usually must do so by swilling Mountain Dew, shouting patriotic slogans, and wearing camo-themed baseball hats before an American public that distrusts intellectuals.

The advisor must then try give smart advice without trying to appear too smart herself. This requires the subtle act of laying out advice in such a way that the person in charge thinks that she came up with the idea herself.

The opening episode of the second season of *Game of Thrones*, titled "The North Remembers" contains a much-commented-upon scene. Cersei Lannister, a character with sinister intent in both the books and HBO series, aspires to be respected as her father had once been. She tires, therefore, of the patronizing aphorisms offered by male advisors. One of these advisors, called Littlefinger, advises Cersei that "knowledge is power."

Piqued by this unwanted advice, Cersei orders her guards to kill Littlefinger. Without delay, the guards raise their weapons and prepare to end Littlefinger's life. Just before the audience gets to see Littlefinger's innards (the audience sees a lot of innards when watching GOT), she orders, "No wait, don't kill him." And then she informs Littlefinger that "power is power."

Subordinates with greater levels of intelligence than their bosses might do well to shade their light. History does not lack for examples of advisors who are stupid enough to believe in the old aphorism that "the pen is mightier than the sword" (whoever said this clearly never held a sword), but two examples of historical subordinates who dared act sincerely should suffice to show the importance of insincerity.

The first example comes from China and involves the Chinese Herodotus, Sima Qian (135–86 BC). Sima worked at the Han Dynasty's court of Emperor Wu as a low-ranking member of the scholar-gentry. Sima had been trained as a writer of histories and as a calendar maker; this meant that Sima spent a lot of time orbiting around the central figure of the emperor.

By the time Sima reached his mid-thirties, his talents brought him to the rank of chief historian and astrologer; this meant that he carried out important bureaucratic functions and even had the occasional opportunity to advise the emperor himself on certain matters.

No record of this exists, but one wonders if proximity to Wu did not make Sima doubt the man's character and intelligence. Subordinates who serve directly with authority figures do not always develop admiration for their bosses.

Something led Sima to either lose respect for the emperor or else led him to overestimate his own relative influence at the court. Although every book with the word *leadership* in the title will likely contain some passage about how important it can be for leaders to listen to honest feedback from employees; all subordinates know that to actually disagree with the boss's idea never really helps anyone's chances for advancement. In modern corporate culture, dissenters might simply be denied promotion, but at the Chinese imperial court in 99 BC, the game of thrones operated under different, and more intense, rules.

In that year, Emperor Wu blamed two generals, one named Li Ling, for a significant defeat against northern barbarians (horse-riding nomads who constantly threatened China's borders). When the emperor pointed a finger of recrimination at someone, the court officials were supposed to raise their fingers and point in the same direction as well, regardless of the circumstances. Sima respected General Li and decided to defend the general publicly in a sincere and courageous display.

Wu saw not courage but insubordination, and he condemned the historian. As punishment, Sima could either pay a fine, die, or lose his penis and testicles to a knife. Sima did not care to die, and his job did not pay the kind of revenue that would be required to pay the fine and save his life or penis. One of the emperor's thugs (one wonders if someone had this as a full-time job or if it came as a special duty) sliced off Sima's manhood, and the historian spent his first three sexless years groveling in a Chinese prison, forced to touch his head to the ground whenever a jailer walked into the cell.

For a member of the scholarly class, castration combined searing pain with professional humiliation. Sima endured all this even though suicide would have been the ordinary reaction from a person of his position who had been so humbled. Sima decided to apply, rather than kill, himself and took up the position of court eunuch at the imperial residence. While there, and seemingly free from sexual distractions or from any other political desires, he wrote *The Records of the Grand Historian*, which is an epic history of China.

At the court of Wu, Sima ranked as a lowly eunuch, but in the eyes of Chinese classicists, he ranks as the highest authority; Chinese history would amount to little more than a blank space filled in periodically by archeological finds without Sima's efforts. Still, one wonders if the man himself would not have preferred to simply have his dick and his old job back.

A little insincerity might have protected Sima's privates. Sima belonged to a time, common throughout most of history until only recently, where authorities governed with the blunt force of direct violence while using Cersei's maxim of "power is power." Nothing controls human behavior more effectively than direct violence and insincerity from authority only evolved in situations where the raw stuff of power cannot be invoked, where authority-as-employer must establish a false front of caring for employees, or where the law provides protection for workers' rights.

Perhaps Sima made the mistake alluded to in the first chapter, that of the feigned retreat or insincere resignation. These cannot be practiced effectively from the subordinate role. Sima did not, as far as anyone knows, threaten to resign his position on principle, but he committed the error's cousin in the sense that he made a political move based on an inflated sense of his own importance.

In all corporations, a subordinate's value is commensurate only to the amount of time and effort it takes to replace him. In other words, the value of a subordinate to authority has almost nothing to do with efficiency or productivity. The hassle of firing and replacing someone is balanced across from every subordinate. The heavier the hassle, the sincerer a subordinate can be without fear of being fired, but this should never be confused with importance.

All of the workplace protections attained through legislation over the years have increased the hassle of firing people, and, in general, the greater the level of seniority an employee has the greater the weight of the documentation required by Human Resources to fire him.

If you, as a senior subordinate, then try a feigned resignation for whatever reason, all you have done is remove all the weight of hassle from the other side of the balance. This means that authority can simply approve your resignation and get someone younger and cheaper who will keep his mouth shut.

Western civilization provides its own example of a Sima Qian; his name was Ancius Boethius (480–524). Boethius practiced the political and philosophical arts among the recent ruins of the Roman Empire. What exactly do historians mean by the idea that Rome collapsed? They tend to date the end to the year 476, when the last ethnic Italian, a boy named Romulus Augustulus, meaning "little Augustus" (very little, as it turned out), stepped down from the throne so that a barbarian German could rule.

This idea that an ethnic-switch-over-equals-the-end-of-empire might sound a little alt-right for more liberal readers, but it's doubtful that late Roman historians intend to engage in any white-on-white racism. The Italians gave way to the Germans and other outlanders who attacked the throne, usually with weapons and supplies the Romans themselves had given them in hopes that the barbarian tribesmen would provide a military defense against all those other scary looking people with axes who drank blood and whooped it up around bonfires on the other side of Rome's borders.

The issue with defining Rome's collapse has to do with a definition. An empire must be centered on a core group, defined by either ethnicity, religion, social class, or nationality. Since Rome was ethnically Italian, the destruction of that core group's control led to the end of the Roman Empire in the same way that when the Mongols took Baghdad in 1258, they ended the Islamic Abbasid Dynasty.

Boethius descended from a long line of imperial big shots. Two of his ancestors wore the emperor's crown, and another one wore the white hat of the pope (just to clarify in case the rhetoric here got too fancy; these ancestors actually were emperors and popes, they did not just put the hats on). Boethius's dad served as a chief advisor to the barbarian emperor of Rome,

Odoacer, but died in the year 487 while Boethius still wandered through childhood.

Shunted to another family of means, Boethius grew up as a privileged orphan and likely found consolation in philosophy for the first time at the age of seven. Grief poured into study can produce excellent powers of concentration, and Boethius starred as a young intellect. He was thirteen in 493, when a barbarian usurper named Theodoric invited Odoacer to a red banquet and, according to Theodoric's own propagandists, hacked a broad sword downward with such force that it bisected Odoacer from neck to groin. That's either hyperbole or a hell of a swing, but the fact that Theodoric approved of the story and its transmission certainly says something about his approach to power.

Bureaucrats tend to ingratiate themselves well with new power structures. In the early days of Arabic conquest and consolidation, the Persians showed their horse-riding, scimitar-swinging new masters how to collect taxes and write up reports.

The Chinese scholar-gentry achieved a similar feat when the Mongols conquered China in the thirteenth century and then did the same again in 1644 when the Manchus rode down from the north and created the Qing Dynasty. After 1945, those Nazi bureaucrats too meager to try for war crimes simply took off the Swastika one day and put on a hammer and sickle the next.

Boethius, too, must have been either untroubled by the hacking death of his dad's former boss, or else so troubled by it that he decided to try and find a job working for Theodoric. Far from being a barbarian thug, Theodoric knew something of philosophy himself as he had taken his learning in Constantinople, where the Greek classics still found respect. He probably knew just enough about philosophy to realize that real power could only be attained politically and through military rule.

Theodoric treated his Roman councilors through the process described earlier, by allowing the bureaucracy to continue its existence. Only a true idiot would ever fire the existing power structure rather than redirect its energies. History gives us one true idiot in George W. Bush, who ordered Paul Bremer to fire the Baathist Iraqi bureaucracy after the orgy of mechanistic slaughter that was the Second Iraq War passed from the shoot-them-into-freedom war phase and into the stand-around-and-be-blown-up occupation phase. George W. Bush was either a stupid criminal or criminally stupid, but Theodoric was not.

Theodoric did, however, proclaim a variation of Christianity considered to be the first variation of heresy. This variation, first proclaimed by the Constantine-era bishop Arius, proclaimed the Nicene Creed, or Holy Trinity, to be a false doctrine on philosophical grounds. Arius stated that a substance could not both be and not be the same as another substance—God, Jesus, and the Holy Ghost could not be the same and different as the bishops who won the vote at the Council of Nicaea declared. Arius, by the way, did not see the insincere purpose of the Nicene Creed.

The Nicene Creed gave priests the opportunity to hold up a mangled piece of logic before the masses and watch as the crowd, with their logical faculties now lobotomized, bow before it. Arius paid for his sincere opposition by suffering assassination through poison so potent that it liquified his intestines, even as a cadre of theocratic murderers liquidated his followers.

Boethius, like all wise men, preferred books to people but entered Theodoric's court nonetheless. He likely felt a duty to use his mind and understood that intellectual cultivation without action to improve society becomes inert. A surgeon who develops her skills for the pleasure of it but refuses to practice in an operating room commits a kind of sin of omission. Such is also true of an intellectual of the Dark Ages; Boethius could not justify leaving governance to crowned outlaws.

The problem, Theodoric found, with coming to power by cleaving someone in half is that it opens up the possibility that the next person who wants to be emperor might feel legitimized in using the same tactic. Theodoric ruled through fear rather than by divine right or through democratic legitimacy. and he proclaimed sincere faith in a creed considered heretical by the religious power structure. The unclear nature of power in the West must have made him even more uneasy.

Did power emanate from Constantinople or from Rome? If both the pope and the emperor derived their powers directly from God, then who trumped whom? It's a doozy of a question, that one, and it vexed Western civilization right up until the Protestant Reformation brought new problems to the fore.

Boethius sincerely believed that Christendom should be held together by a singular belief system; he sympathized not at all with Arianism. Even worse, he preferred to keep the West's allegiance to Constantinople rather than Rome. A proper Byzantine emperor appealed to him more than the sword-wielding German who occupied the Western chair. To further incite Theodoric, the Byzantine East fired up a persecution of Arians in a pre-Inquisition bout of heretic hunting. Boethius caught Theodoric's nervous rage when he defended a bishop who'd sent a letter to Constantinople that contained some type of sentiment at which Theodoric took offense.

No one makes more enemies than a sincere and intelligent bureaucrat, and Boethius made plenty. His rivals cupped their hands around the ear of Theodoric and whispered condemnations. The barbarian king bullied the Roman Senate into decreeing Boethius a criminal, and they then sentenced the philosopher to death. Barbarian kings like Theodoric cared little for either the eye-scooping/nose slicing theatrics of the Byzantine court or for the penis-and-testes-hacking tactics of the Far East. Boethius lingered in an Italian prison and kept his mind off things by writing *The Consolation of Philoso-*

phy. Boethius belonged to a different era where educated people read the same texts over and over, so his memory of the great works allowed him to quote them directly from his mind. Theodoric's thugs beat him to death in the year 524.

In his book, Boethius talks with a character named Lady Philosophy. Boethius wondered, as we all would if we found ourselves awaiting a certain and painful death, whether providence or chance led him to this sordid fate. Philosophy tells him "Wherever something is done for some purpose, and for certain reason, something other than what was intended happens, it is called chance." When this is planned, of course, it is called "insincerity."

These two examples of sincere court philosophers and advisors show the dangers of sincerity. The outcome of an action changes our view of the action. Here's a question worth pondering: Would Socrates and Jesus still be considered heroes if their actions led them, as Sima Qian's did, to castration rather than suicide or crucifixion? What if Jesus had to live out his days as a eunuch? It's kind of sexy to be crucified for one's beliefs at age thirty-three but less heroic by many degrees to live as a castrate for decades until dying of natural causes.

Nonetheless, these two examples of smarty-pantses acting as sincere advisors to power show the perils of sincerity in a less enlightened time. In modern corporate culture, punishments tend to be less severe, and disciplinary actions tend to involve the taking of dignity, a process that involves reprimanding the subordinate in such a way that it reduces self-esteem and reminds the subordinate of his inferior position.

Yet, still, the words that get used for getting rid of someone in a corporation sound like wistful euphemisms for bygone days when someone in power could actually kill a subordinate. Someone is "fired" from a job, or his position gets "terminated." The former word is derived from the concept of the firing squad. and the latter is a word that means to kill or destroy.

"Firing" someone might not be as good as killing someone from a superior's position, but the corporate connotation is the same. When people disappear from the workplace, when they are fired or terminated, this amounts to professional death. Sometimes people are allowed to resign, which is like committing suicide in lieu of an impending execution.

The psychological problem involving sincerity and insincerity might result from an underestimation of the power of torture. Both Sima and Boethius made courageous gestures, and surely this prevented the immediate force of frustration from seizing up their stomachs, but at that point neither could have balanced that frustration against the pain of castration or of a jail-cell beat-down.

Likewise, an employee who fails to hold back the frustration of being subordinate, and issues sincere declarations that lead to being fired, might not foresee the pain of unemployment. Once one sees the knives, or the shadow of imperial thugs in the doorway of the jail cell, or the long months of self-esteem-destroying unemployment, insincerity and frustration might seem the better option in hindsight.

With this stated, the classical paragon of subordinate insincerity is Procopius, and the great classical book of insincerity, his *The Secret History*. In order to understand Procopius, a bit of historical context need be applied. After the Roman west collapsed in 476, the eastern empire lived on and now goes by the historical title of Byzantium. The word *byzantine* lives on, usually used by one of the upper-tier news organizations, always in a pejorative sense, as a bureaucratic descriptor. For example, "The CIA failed to share information with the FBI because information got lost in the byzantine network of offices."

The Byzantine Empire housed a powerful scholarly elite that supposedly squashed innovation and capitalism. The Byzantines spoke Greek rather than Latin and tended to regard the pope's claims to authority with something ranging between skepticism and hostility.

Procopius, probably born around the year 500, entered into the Byzantine court around the year 527. The education of Byzantine officials involved the secular classics handed down from the ancient Greeks as well as a study of biblical works. Although it's difficult to define his job as it existed in the specific Byzantine concept, he functioned as a lawyer and shared advice with the general Belisarius.

The job of a general in this time period involved ordering people to stab pointy objects into the bodies of outlanders, and Belisarius embraced this aspect of the profession. Procopius followed his boss into the Middle East, Africa, and even into Italy where the Byzantines still held ambitions of uniting the eastern and western sections of the empire into one power structure.

Let's get this point out of the way right from the very beginning. Procopius served at the court of Justinian and Theodora, and when not on campaign, he wrote what he was told to write. The "official" works ascribed to him go by the titles of *The Histories* and *Buildings*. In glaring contrast to Sima and Boethius, Procopius not only avoided physical mutilation and public humiliation but also managed to be celebrated in his time. Late in his life, he even earned the title of *illustris* (Latin for "kind of a big deal") and died, wealthy and respected, of natural causes in the year 565.

Yet, his actions before Justinian and Theodora could have been nothing but insincere as he left behind *The Secret History*, and this can be read now in editions published by Penguin Classics (a few side words: Penguin Classics will one day be recognized as the savior of civilization. It makes the great works of humanity available for the few people whose intellects remain free from the screened prison of social media). This lengthy passage about Procopius comes from the introduction to the 1966 edition, and is written by

G. A. Williamson, and its inclusion is justified because what he writes clearly cannot be improved upon:

> Why was *The Secret History* written but not published? And why is it so extraordinarily different from the author's other works that some have doubted whether it could have been written by the same man? The Histories, which were to win such high commendation from Gibbon, are careful, methodical, chronological, and accurate records of a series of wars, in which tribute is paid to the genius and high character of the commander-in-chief, and no aspersions are cast either on him or his wife, or his imperial employers. The Secret History, which professes to be an extension of the first seven of the books of The Histories, and begins with sentences which appear to link it with the end of Book VII, is a ferocious diatribe against all four and against many of the Emperor's officials, exposing mercilessly both their public actions and their private lives, and stripping them bare of any claim to admiration or even common respect. From start to finish it is an unpleasant book; some would say horrid. No one who reads it will feel much doubt as to why it was not published. If a fraction of the charges which it levels against the Emperor and Empress are true, imagination boggles at the thought of what would have happened to the author had they ever known that he had written such things about them. The question is not why it was not published but why it was written at all. Was it, as some have suggested, merely a letting off of steam, a boiling over of spleen and spite in a man disgruntled because he was denied promotion? I think not. I believe that knowing that his earlier writing had left much unsaid, though they were truthful and sober history as far as they went and were written in the only way that would make publication possible in a time of tyranny and terror, Procopius felt that the other side of the truth must be set forth too, and expressed with a vehemence and starkness that strike us as extravagant and in bad taste. In his view monstrous crimes must be laid bare with brutal frankness. (Williamson, in Procopius 1966 [reprint], 27–28)

Piqued at the royal treatment of his general and friend, Belisarius, Procopius chose not to be a hero. Instead he wrote:

> Belisarius, although none of the charges was brought home to him, was at the instigation of the Empress deprived by the Emperor of the command which he held, and replaced by Martin as general in the East. . . . Many of his friends and other old helpers were forbidden to associate with Belisarius any more. A pitiful sight and an incredible spectacle, Belisarius went about as a private citizen in Byzantium, almost alone, always gloomy and melancholy, in continual fear of death by a murderer's hand. Learning that he had accumulated great wealth in the East, the Empress sent one of the Palace eunuchs to bring it all to her. (Procopius 1966 [reprint], 57)

This does not read like a story made up for purposes of character assassination. Procopius clearly hated his bosses, as he makes clear later in this passage, "What sort of people were Justinian and Theodora? And how did it come about that they destroyed the greatness of Rome? These are questions I must answer next." With that endorsement, Procopius goes on to describe Justinian's intellectual capabilities late in life:

> [H]e was by now a doddering old man, totally illiterate—in popular parlance, he didn't know his ABC—an unheard of thing in a Roman. It was the invariable custom that the Emperor should append his own signature to all documents embodying decrees drafted by him. Justin, however, was incapable of either drafting his own decrees or taking an intelligent interest in the measures contemplated. . . . On a short strip of polished wood they cut a stencil in the shape of four letters spelling the Latin for I HAVE READ. Then they used to dip a pen in the special ink reserved for emperors and place it in the hands of the Emperor Justin. Next they took a strip of wood described above and laid it on the document, grasped the Emperor's hand, and while he held the pen guided it along the pattern of the four letters, taking it round all the bends cut in the wooden stencil. (1966 [reprint], 69–70)

Try to imagine a more damning image of anyone. Was Justinian this stupid and crippled, or was Procopius exaggerating, or did Justinian develop Alzheimer's in his old age? Who knows? Procopius later writes:

> The plague, as I mentioned in an earlier volume, fell upon the whole world; yet just as many people escaped as had the misfortune to succumb—either because they escaped infection altogether, or because they got over it if they happened to be infected. But this man not a single person in the whole Roman Empire could escape: like any other visitation from heaven falling on the entire human race he left no one completely untouched. Some he killed without any justification; others he reduced to penury, making them even more wretched than those who had died. In fact, they begged him to put an end to their misery by any death however painful. Some he deprived of their possession and of life as well. But it gave him no satisfaction merely to ruin the Roman Empire: he insisted on making himself master of Libya and Italy for the sole purpose of destroying their inhabitants along with those already subject to him. (1966 [reprint], 71)

Procopius is to insincerity what Shakespeare was to the stage. *The Secret History* ranks as the defining classic of the insincerity genre, and Procopius's biographical success is enduring proof of the usefulness of insincerity. This brings us to a pertinent philosophical and ethical question: Does the ethical responsibility to do or live by all the things exhorted by junior high motivational posters, i.e., "do the right thing" "what is popular is not always right and what is right is not always popular" become more incumbent upon the individual as the punishments become less severe? Procopius failed to stand up and defend Belisarius, even though his writings clearly indicate that his heart pulled him to do so.

Logically speaking, in that situation, to stand up to Belisarius would simply increase the harm done by authority. The situation for Belisarius would unlikely change while men with knives might have done nasty things to Procopius. Insincerity in such a situation would seem ethically suitable. However, when the penalty for sincerity merely involves the denial of promotion, what can be considered ethical? Is there a sliding scale? As the penalty for insincerity becomes more painful, does it become more ethical to act insincerely?

In an era where discussions of totalitarianism seemed more relevant, Hannah Arendt wrote that totalitarian regimes became vulnerable only when the government attempted to reform. Military terror and overwhelming central force work pretty well for keeping people down.

This may be because as the penalties for sincerity slide down the scale during a "thaw" or period of reform, then it becomes more likely for subordinates to act sincerely. If enough people act with sincerity, then the system itself can be overthrown. This concept of measuring sincerity and insincerity among equals, and the way in which ethics can be determined through these means, will be developed in the next chapter.

For students, particularly for those who have never held a job, the idea of insincerity being enforced by the power structure might be alarming. Hypersensitive millennials, sometimes called "snowflakes" because of their fragility, do not consider themselves subordinates.

Snowflakes define themselves as customers, and customers are in the business of consumption. These perpetual adolescents consume education and then consume the honors and awards that are associated with education. Sometimes, for balance, they consume experiences, and these can range from weekend ski trips to a semester spent in "service learning" working in faraway places with deep poverty.

This inability to see themselves as subordinates might be what leads to the most bizarre feature of modern public life: authority-approved protests. The best example of this comes from the fall of 2017, when President Trump essentially declared Sunday to be Trumpday by declaring, in an Alabama speech supporting a Senate candidate and again through a series of Tweets, that NFL players who kneeled during the national anthem should be fired. He mentioned nothing about the high-profile cases involving police violence against African Americans that supposedly caused the original protest by Colin Kaepernick of the San Francisco 49ers.

Trump wanted the NFL authorities to crack down on their subordinates. The problem with this is that, in doing so, the president treated the NFL team owners as if they themselves were subordinates. The NFL authorities, being the owners, did not want to be seen as the president's subordinates and so they joined their players in protests-lite that suddenly involved kneeling before the anthem and then standing for it.

The originator of this shock-value movement that did nothing to help the cause, the aforementioned Kaepernick, possessed no special talent as an actual athlete and even less as a spokesperson. Watching someone kneel during the national anthem induces nausea because it immediately equates a general symbol for the positive with specific support for the negative, but at least our unremarkable athlete did not ask permission. People stand for the anthem as a temporary reprieve from political divisiveness and as a show of unity and respect for a few basic higher ideals. Ethically, the national anthem and the American flag should be off-limits for any kind of degradation.

The NFL's corporate leaders found themselves trapped. For years, they had force-fed their fan base manufactured patriotism by "honoring" the military with showy halftime extravaganzas. These shows, by the way, hardly turned out to be deep displays of affection as the military secretly paid the NFL to put them on. Now, these same leaders, when confronted with a man kneeling under the weight of his afro, had no idea how to respond. Fire him and risk upsetting the black men who make up the majority of the NFL, or let him continue to play and potentially nurse resentment in a large portion of their fans?

The NFL did nothing except let the player's contract run out. No one would hire Kaepernick because he might drive away a percentage of the fan base, and soon enough, Trump called out the NFL on its insincerity. Good, by the way, for him. Trump has a repulsive side, but one tires of presidents who pretend to be above the fray when the entire point of being a politician is to be in it.

Then, Kaepernick, who supposedly knew what he was kneeling for, managed to spread his protest to so many players that the only real authority in the situation, the NFL owners and league president, ended up *sanctioning* the rebellion. Only this time the rebellion was against . . . well, no one knows. A player who protested police brutality by protesting a symbol of the United States somehow caused a series of millionaires to link arms with multimillionaires to protest against an American president exercising his rights to free speech.

Malcolm X once called Martin Luther King's famous March on Washington a "Farce on Washington," because the very authorities that were supposed to be threatened by the movement co-opted it. Soon enough, the authorities zoned the marches and directed the traffic. If they cared so much about Dr. King, one wonders why more was not done to protect his life in the following days. What good is a revolutionary who begins the rebellions by asking the authorities, "Can we protest?"

People who proclaim a liberal political bent, especially, delight in making meaningless social-media stands regarding tragic events in the world. This sometimes involves holding up placards that call for the return of African girls stolen by African Islamists, and sometimes it involves sending canned goods to someplace or another to help with disaster relief. None of it helps anybody very much, but it advertises to one's peers that one stands on the right side of history.

This silliness might not be quite benign as it sometimes seeps into foreign affairs. Foreign affairs, as an arena, requires that politicians arm themselves with realpolitik rather than insincere slogans. One can only eagerly await a time when American leftists decide that an appropriate answer to Russian aggressiveness in central Asia will be to link arms in Seattle and shout to the northwest "You're all racist" at our Asiatic political provocateurs.

This last example about insincerity from insubordinates will hopefully not date this book. Rather, it should act as an example of how any particular event-of-the-moment might be examined by analyzing the role of insincerity. Teachers and professors might pull any event from the mouths of attractive news-bots and design a lesson about insincerity around it.

KEY POINTS

- The pen is not mightier than the sword. Subordinates who are smarter than their superiors would do well to study the effects that acting with sincerity had on Sima Qian and Boethius. They fared less well than the Byzantine historian Procopius, who wrote the classic of insincerity.
- George Orwell's *1984* got the concept of insincerity wrong because authority loses power when subordinates become true believers. Real power exists when authority can force subordinates to feel one way but act another; the goal is to enforce insincere action not to create sincere belief.
- *Catch-22* offers a better analysis of how insincerity from authority creates cynicism in subordinates.
- Martin Luther refused to issue an insincere recantation in 1521 and created a bloody era of religious sincerity. Less than a decade later, Galileo issued an insincere apology and recantation to the Catholic authorities rather than suffer and die. What's so great about sincerity?
- Sincerity from subordinates becomes an ethical requirement only in cases where authority does not employ direct terror and violence. In cases where authority holds that kind of power, acting sincerely as a subordinate might be idiotic.

Chapter Three

Insincerity among Equals

"Hell is other people," wrote Jean Sartre, with appropriate existential angst. With this quote, he encapsulated a sentiment about human beings that highlights the frustration of social living. Sartre meant that each person views other people as reflections of impressions. We try, all of us, to impress an image of ourselves on others and, when the impression of ourselves fails to get reflected, when others fail to see us brilliant, or tough, or pretty, or pious, the result becomes an overwhelming frustration. Hell.

Everyone else views you, too, as a potential means for reflecting an image of themselves. Spouses, children, colleagues, and friends, through hundreds of daily interactions, demonstrate that others perceive us differently than we perceive ourselves by refusing to recognize the status that each of us wishes that we had.

Occasionally, circumstances create a situation where others must pretend to see us as we wish they always did and special events get constructed for the purpose of co-opting everyone into a mass of insincere display. Weddings, funerals, and award ceremonies all function to force others into insincere displays of happiness, grief, or respect.

Weddings, with their formalized procedures, require rehearsals so that everyone present can bring the proper attitude of respect and reverence to the proceedings. A wedding represents one of the few times in life when two people, through the force of the moment, can force societal equals to stand at attention and reflect the emotions and attitudes toward them that they wish to see.

The couple themselves, exhausted with planning and forced to swallow any dissatisfaction with either the lifelong mate, cost of the ceremony, or wisdom of the whole marital enterprise must smile for pictures and pretend to enjoy having icing rubbed on the tips of their noses. Need the insincerity of the virginal white dress even be mentioned?

This insincerity on display is necessary so that the audience can get the big payoff—not basking in the happiness of others—but free food and cheap or free booze at the reception. No one wants to be at the actual ceremony and everyone but the Catholics realize this, so the insincere ceremony usually lasts only a short time. The audience won't tolerate it.

The same is true, by the way, of any religious service anywhere. No one wants to go to church and most don't. Those who do think of the whole dismal process as a way of stuffing time into a celestial retirement account, hoping somehow that God will accept an hour and a half of discomfort once a week as an acceptable contribution for an eternal pension.

Little children wriggling in their Sunday clothes can think only of ripping them off and running around in sincere freedom. Probably, once, women who never had an opportunity to dress up and leave the house may have enjoyed the chance to show off their fabric plumage on a Sunday morning, but who wants to put on nice clothes for God when the boss has demanded it all week? Old ladies go to church mostly to see other old ladies.

No one wants to honor the dead. Funerals serve to enrich the living who specialize in the art of practiced insincerity, who have mastered the peculiar profession of filling the veins of corpses with embalming fluid or of burning off the carbon in a living body so that all that remains is a transformed clump that can fit into a little brass receptacle. The dead don't care.

In the nineteenth century, a certainly common fantasy made its way into literature—the idea of attending one's own funeral. The conceit being that some accident occurred that made a person's death certain but produced no corpse, and that the "dead" person would show up to hear all the nice words said about him and then reveal himself to be really alive. Mark Twain conjured up this scenario in *Tom Sawyer*.

Funerals and weddings share this in common; friends, families, or colleagues can suddenly, through the raw force of emotion, make other people react to their own family and selves in a way acceptable to the people at center stage. Attendees must think: "You are so happy in your relationship that you are going to have a ceremony and your reward is that everyone will act the way you want them to." Or, "You are so sad over a death that everyone will gather and act the way you want them to." In both cases, the guests still expect catering and, at some point, reciprocation.

Award ceremonies are the only other kind of event analogous to weddings and funerals. Extreme emotions and extraordinary achievement can force colleagues and other "equals" into a position where they must reflect your own image of yourself. No one wants to see someone else honored; everyone in the audience of an award ceremony would beam with perfect delight if the honoree got arrested for drunk driving or caught with some inappropriate pornography on his computer.

Millennials will never know the joys that once came from the scandalous discovery that some person of acquaintance preferred the company of a sexual sort from someone of the same gender—now the scandal would be the notion that it's a scandal. Social progress this may be, but let us take a moment to close our eyes in memory of what it was once like to savor the delicious dish of disgrace through deviant sexuality, however ill-defined. Public disgrace trumps public dishonor every time in the public scandal.

Most awards serve an interesting function; they elevate a colleague slightly above her equals, but the process of application for the award renders the whole process insincere. The applicant must marshal letters of recommendation, fill out an application, and more or less provide the means by which the awards-hander-outers can vet that they aren't giving a trophy to a crazy person. The fact that the whole mess probably distracts the nominee from whatever important work she should be engaged in never gets mentioned.

Most times, the people who write the recommendation letters will ask the applicant herself to write the recommendation letter! The book *Dear Committee Members* by Julie Schumacher parodies the cult of Recommendation Letter Writing by crafting a novel out of nothing but letters of recommendation (LORs) written by an English professor. One excerpt captures the insincerity of writing recommendations:

> Feel free to contact me for further information via phone or email. And forgive the brevity of this letter. I do believe that student writing speaks for itself, and though the academic year has just started, I fear I am already losing a never-ending battle to catchup with the recommendations requested of me. Suffice it to say that the LOR has usurped the place of my own work, now adorned with cobwebs and dust in a remote corner of my office. (2015, 10–11)

Professors write insincere recommendations that no one ever reads, for students who only serve to impress professors so that they can procure letters of recommendation.

Organizations that supply awards generally do so as a justification for their own existence. There is tall stack of mediocre books that can claim "Pulitzer Prize"–winning status despite being considered minor works in comparison to nonwinners like *The Catcher in the Rye* or *Catch-22*. The stated purpose of the Pulitzer may be to reward excellence in letters, but all committees that mint metals, hammer out plaques, or bestow status must do so in the hopes that the honorees' rise in status gets reflected back on the committee.

Individuals in corporations of any kind do a job really well, generally, only in an attempt to raise personal status. The desire for personal status in an organization facilitates the development of two separate hierarchies. The official hierarchy promotes individuals from below—delegating a former equal to a superior status. Sometimes the promotion might be a reward for genuine competency, although competency might just be a secondary-rider to promotions that are subject to the laws of probability. Promote enough people, and some will exhibit traits of competency.

When individuals get promoted through the official hierarchy, this creates a separate hierarchy of resentment. Those who do not rise create a hierarchy where the assumption is that their failure to be promoted can be attributed both to their own personal sincerities and to the insincerities of those who did get promotions.

People in the hierarchy of resentment assert, usually in whispers, that the newly promoted are ass-kissers, brownnosers, bootlickers, and suck-ups. In other words, the promoted act insincerely only for the purpose of gaining promotion in a hierarchy that rewards that type of behavior. People tend to end up on one hierarchy or another mostly by accident, and people in the hierarchy of resentment might switch columns upon landing a new job.

Insincerity for sex borders someone between clever and criminal, and surely predates human society. In *The Descent of Man*, Darwin wrote of insincere displays of a battle between male birds for the purpose of impressing females:

> In the case of Tetrao umbellus, a good observer goes so far as to believe that the battles of the males "are all a sham, performed to show themselves to the greatest advantage before the admiring females who assemble around; for I have never been able to find a maimed hero and seldom more than a broken feather." (2006 [reprint], 1050)

Insincerity for sex brings up a series of increasingly complex ethical questions. Does a man or woman who feigns emotional interest in a partner for the purpose of procuring sexual activity commit an unethical act? Does a transgender person, say a person who "identifies" as female while possessing male genitalia, need to disclose this information to a potential partner before engaging in an act of sexuality?

Is it, in an era when fragile collegians might be triggered if someone assumes hisher gender, still okay to inquire whether the person who is about to engage in sexual activity is a man, woman, or something else? That, sincerely, is where the logic ends up.

None of this matters, of course. The purpose of gender-neutrality or "cisgender" politics, whatever, has little to do with logic or equality. Civil rights activism gets good coverage in universities and the liberal press—students who fancy themselves as modern-day Martin Luther Gandhis because they march for cisgender equality really just want to draw attention to their own self-righteousness. It's probably easier than learning physics anyway.

To return to the earlier point, the external manifestation of genes depends upon the environment, a fact that renders so much of the speculation from evolutionary psychology inert. Imagine seeing someone swimming in a pond. One might speculate as to why the physical equipment—the rotator cuffs and opposable thumbs used for cupped palms, and such—that allowed for the person to swim evolved in the first place.

To speculate that the person's ancestors must have evolved in the pond itself would be erroneous. The reason why is immediately understandable. Imagine the same person throwing a baseball. You could then speculate that the exact same physical equipment, the rotator cuffs and opposable thumbs, must have evolved for that trait.

Biologically speaking, the rotator cuff and opposable thumb almost certainly evolved from *australopithecine*, an arboreal human ancestor from roughly seven million years ago. Thumbs and rotator cuffs, still a feature of the tree-dwelling monkeys that share so much of our anatomy, almost certainly evolved for swinging through trees.

The environment shaped rotator cuffs and opposable thumbs for living in trees, but the expression of those same genes in a different environment (i.e., a swimming pool or baseball field) gives the genes a different purpose. The biological term for this is exaptation, sometimes called pre-adaptation, and can be seen everywhere in animal anatomy or technology. A turtle "walks" slowly, to use another example, because it is using swim fins for walking on land.

This leads us to the question: "Is it natural to fake a smile? Was the ability to fake smiles or feign excitement directly shaped in hunter-gatherer society? Anthropologists have identified smiles and laughter as being a commonality across all human cultures; and humor likely helps connect members of a community. Almost every trait that defines civilization involves the domestication of a process that once occurred randomly in the wild. Human observers captured the process then artificially replicated it so as to control it.

For example, Jared Diamond has argued that farming probably evolved from human latrines. People who settled in one region for a period of time likely created a specific place to defecate; this would have passed seeds through the intestinal system into fertilized ground. Once food-bearing plants sprouted from this ground, humans could decipher the code for growing food in a single place. Likewise, unexpected events tend to make people expel air in short huffs while escalating dopamine levels.

A hunter-gatherer who tripped on a rock while hunting and gathering and cracked his nuts on a tree stump probably elicited laughs from his comrades. Anyone wanting to replicate the situation could then insincerely trip at a later time in the hopes of replicating the laughter that went along with the original situation. Unexpected occurrences generate laughter, so the deliberate attempt to create a situation where an unexpected event can occur—setting something up so that it looks to have one purpose but actually has another—constitutes humor.

This is why the straight man plays such an important part in humor. A dour-looking gent in a suit looks like he wants to convey some important information about medical insurance. However, the real purpose of the setup is to lull the audience into a stupor so that the eventual impact of the cream pie in the man's face will cause greater convulsions of laughter.

American audiences spend so much time consuming contrived comedic situations that they are hard to fool, and this might be why so many comedies fail to be comedic and why so many comedians must settle for polite giggles: the act of advertising the comedy ruins the premise. The audience knows they are there to be surprised as the comic reveals her insincerity.

There are a few ways to address this. The first, most common Hollywood approach is to simply abandon the notion of being funny altogether and strive to make the audience feel moderately amused for an hour or so. Most comedic movies follow some variation of this theme: (1) a gang of ne'er-do-wells begin the movie by doing ne'er-do-well types of activities; (2) they suddenly discover a good cause that they need to make money for (saving something, usually); and (3) they contrive some whacky way to make the money.

Count the number of comedies that follow this premise and the tears that flow won't be from laughter—even variations of the theme can be depressing. The 2008 film *Be Kind Rewind*, featuring Jack Black and some other people, put a couple of guys in a position where they are trying to remake VHS movies like *Robocop* or *Rush Hour 2* on a budget.

The movie's plot alters from the ne'er-do-wells trying to remake accidentally erased tapes before the store owner (Danny Glover) returns home, to trying to make enough money with their homemade remakes to save the store. In this case, the ne'er-do-wells fail to bring in enough cash to keep the old place going, but the community comes together as a result of the movie-making. It serves as proof that imaginative twists on the genre never get too imaginative.

On-stage comedians, there to be funny in front of an audience who paid for it, must abandon the surprise-as-humor construct and try to gradually raise dopamine levels in the audience members by drawing them into stories with surprise twists, often involving puns. A pun-joke example might be "I woke up this morning and found a post-it note on the refrigerator door from my wife. It said, 'this isn't working, good-bye.' I don't know what she's talking about because I opened the door and the fridge is working fine."

At one time, television audiences could apparently be shocked into laughter without much thought. Milton Berle dressed as a woman produced such a shock in the audience that one woman can be heard hyperventilating in hysterics.

In the 1980s, with the advent of home video cameras, studio executives could once again bring a sincere humor out to the world. With millions of people aiming cameras at their friends and family, people are bound to get mildly injured when they fail to understand the physics behind a slip n' slide and somehow end up on the highway, or when a father holding a piñata gets whacked in the nads by some four-year-old who is juiced up on cupcake icing and undue attention. This makes for simply great television and *America's Funniest Home Videos* (*AFV*) has run steadily for over thirty years for a reason. The comedic setups are sincere.

The problem here, of course, is that, by offering money to those who send in comedic situations involving pain, the producers of *AFV* provide an incentive for amateurs to try and game the system by creating their own comedic situations. *AFV* only traffics in sincere setups and mild injuries: so thumbs up for a piñata stick in the nuts, but thumbs down for an accidental beheading on a roller-coaster ride. The severity of the injury determines whether we respond with laughter or horror; and when someone falls in a gray zone, we tend to respond by laughing and then saying, with insincerity, "Are you okay?"

It's no great insight to see the similarity between humor and horror; both depend upon the insincere setup and suffer from the same problem. One must advertise the setup in order to attract followers, revealing the whole process to be false, which takes away the opportunity to feel real fear. Horror movies can respond to this in a few ways; the first was to create fantastic tales that did not so much elicit fear in the audience as a morbid interest.

A cinematic trick that often gets employed for eliciting surprise/fear in the audience involves setting up a scene where an individual, usually a slightly postadolescent female in revealing clothing, hears a noise in some secluded place and decides to investigate. Instrumental music escalates the tension as the girl walks into a dark and secluded place.

Then a cat jumps out! The source of the noise discovered, our heroine relaxes and laughs. Presumably, the audience relaxes as well, but then the nubile lady-girl turns right into the psychopath and gets hacked up or power-drilled, or whatever. The situation lures the audience into a brief moment of respite, where the attack becomes suddenly unexpected, thus recreating the feeling of fear as it exists in the "wild."

This trick only works once or twice, which is why these are movies about postadolescents for postadolescents. It's also why the other variation of horror movie, involving an hour and a half of dingy scenes and graphic images of torture, tend to do away with the tactic. It's unclear why anyone watches any of it, but the movies get cut cheaply and draw massive crowds so it is clear why they get made. Another new favorite is the "found footage" horror film, supposedly depicting live events by someone who refuses to put down a camera and run.

Societal equals sometimes try to take advantage of unsuspecting friends or colleagues by playing pranks. A common theme of the prank involves setting up the stooge while he sleeps, or by putting saran wrap over the doorway. The point is to humiliate some unsuspecting dupe and then to record it for uploading on YouTube.

MTV, a prime contributor to the collapse of civilization ever since it started pimping irresponsibility as a means to fame, churns out shows that feature elaborate pranking routines. Apparently, there's a market.

Curse words function in much the same way that jokes do. One would think that shouting "shit!" after banging your shins on something would be one of the sincerest acts a person could commit, and maybe it is, but the social function of curse words is to determine status in the hierarchy. What, exactly, makes something a "bad" word? Why do children get punished for using a lexicon that adults throw around all the time without any seemingly negative social effects?

The N-word brings with it a special connotation as it functions like a secret handshake within the African American community. Casually used in conversation and music by and between African American friends, the word functions as a societal probe. White people who use the word commit a social sin equivalent to telling a deviant-sex joke to a grandmother's garden club.

For a non-black person, acquiring an "N-word" pass means that one is so free of racism, by virtue of having so many African American friends or a black significant other, that one has permission from the African American community to use the word! A word that once showed the speaker to be racist now indicates, in some instances, that the non-black speaker is so free of racism that he has earned the right to use it.

No word can be inherently wrong, but the social construct around the word makes it "bad." People tend to only use curse words around other people of equal standing. Ten-year-old boys might spew curses and filth around each other but speak with eloquent innocence around parents and teachers.

A child who speaks around authority like he speaks around his peers assumes a relationship of equality with the authority and *this*, and not the word, constitutes the sin. One can test the boundaries of equality in a relationship by gradually evolving a filthier mouth around friends or colleagues. Close friends can speak with scatological humor that becomes offensive out of context.

Curse words, rather than actually functioning as nouns, verbs, or exclamations, are actually societal probes used to determine how equal people are in status. This is the insincerity inherent in their usage. Men might use scatological humor with each other as a means of testing equal status in such a way that might baffle the opposite sex, and not all men do this, but the dirtier the words and the humor the closer the assumed relationship.

The most famous political event involving scatological humor came just before the 2016 elections. Donald Trump, before he became president of the United States, told a television tabloid reporter about his attempt at a sexual exploit with a blonde and leggy journalist. Trump's words got recorded by the microphone that he and the esteemed journalist Billy Bush happened to be wearing.

When all this got to the press, the poor innocents in the media practically fainted dead away. Morally upstanding senators, many of whom regularly vote to use U.S. military power to just slaughter the hell out people in developing countries for some manufactured reason or another, blushed and condemned.

Yet, the public recovered, probably because the public recognized that Trump was not actually describing an attempted sexual assault but was really trying to project an image onto Billy Bush. What was that image? "Hey, I'm famous and a big deal but I will sit here and talk to you like we are equals." Billy Bush seemed flattered by all of the equality being splattered onto him. Donald Trump's wife, with her perpetual "I just really need to concentrate on reading this cereal box" facial expression, seemed untroubled, which is probably why she's Donald Trump's wife.

In the workplace, men know intrinsically that they may never use scatological humor with female colleagues. A woman might toss out a zinger about PMS, or even make a sex joke, but she must do so before the men. The point is not the joke, but to signal to her male colleagues that she is not "one of *those* women." She does not suffer from perpetual aggrievement.

The desire to not be one of *those* women sometimes gets pushed to the edges. The thriller novel and movie *Gone Girl* depicts a sociopathic woman in rage against men. The main character, Amy Dunne, swallowed the "cool girl" stereotype, swilling beer and pretending to care about sports and video games, in exchange for male companionship that hardly seemed worth it. She then got her revenge in a brilliant way, by trapping her perpetually adolescent husband into family life with her; she becomes a killer insincerely living as a victim, and he a boy insincerely living as a man.

In 1979, W. J. Rorabaugh published *The Alcoholic Republic: An American Tradition* where he stated, "Americans between 1790 and 1830 drank more alcoholic beverages per capita than ever before or since" (p. ix). Why? Rorabaugh indicates that the alcohol may have been less important than the message that getting drunk together sent about equality:

> Militiamen elected their officers with the expectation that the elected officers would treat. One newly elevated colonel pledged, "I can't make a speech, but what I lack in brains I will try and make up in rum." Voters demanded and received spirits in exchange for their ballots. Electoral success, explained one Kentucky politico, depended upon understanding that *"the way to men's hearts*

> *is, down their throats."* At trials the bottle was passed among spectators, attorneys, clients—and to the judge. If the foreman of the jury became mellow in his cups, the defendant stood an excellent chance for acquittal.
>
> Alcohol was pervasive in American society; it crossed regional, sexual, racial, and class lines. (1979, 20)

Getting drunk may be sincere, but the act of requesting that someone else drink to excess forces a sense of equality on the other in the same way that telling a dirty joke does. By refusing to drink or refusing to laugh, you are indicating a superiority to the other person and therefore an unwillingness to engage with him as an equal.

Even Joseph Stalin, who used to keep his politburo "comrades" (Stalin routinely kept their wives in prison) up for all-night drinking bouts, was reported to substitute water for vodka. Stalin's all-night bouts of comraderies were as much for show as the public trials of reported dissidents.

In the modern workplace, people can't binge on vodka or corn squeezin's without jeopardizing their employment status. American men gauge each other's equal status through sports talk. Europeans who travel to the United States, particularly if they get to the center parts, often report being rather taken aback by American friendliness. Speak with a thick enough accent, particularly an Irish brogue or good south London cockney, and Americans will brighten up and ask you what part of Australia you are from.

In his memoir *Hitch-22*, Christopher Hitchens wrote that the American propensity for chatting about sports and the weather rather perplexed him at first until he realized that inquiries into the weather or the local sports team's seasonal success or lack thereof were really insincerities of a positive sort. When someone asks you what you thought of last night's game or what you think of the oppressive heat or cold outside, she is really offering up an invitation to converse pleasantly as an equal. It's a charming custom.

Except for when it takes over. Michael Kimmel, in his book *Guyland: The Perilous World Where Guys Become Men*, describes the world of white men in their early twenties (a few attempts are made to explore beyond this in African American culture, but Kimmel's clear interest is with middle-class frat boys and their ilk). Sports talk dominates the lives of these boys, but not because anyone is really interested, just because it provides a social cohesive and a shared sense of vocabulary. The same goes for hooking up with college girls; the act of bragging about sex provides a status bump with the boys—so even sex is insincere.

It can be insincere for young women, too. Lots of young men and women, particularly those from religious homes, think that avoiding a single kind of penetrative sexual act, while engaging in all of the other kinds of sexual acts, makes them "virgins."

Adults should not overthink the sex lives of younger people, but the notion that oral, anal, and manual sex somehow don't count as acts that take away one's virginity smells insincere. Lesbians with long sexual histories could call themselves virgins under this auspice, although they probably would not want to.

This points to another issue. No woman ever asked a potential mate about his one-rep max at the bench press. Young men lift weights to impress other men. Ladies probably do appreciate a little muscle tone, but young men who record their personal best on the deadlift do so to impress other young men, so the whole process becomes another means of insincerity—boys pumping up their muscles for the stated purpose of impressing girls really do so for the purpose of impressing other boys.

Such must be the case with all sports as well. Surely people cannot be so stupid as to find entertainment in the spectacle of enormous men only recently released from adolescence either slamming into one another (very popular), throwing a ball into a hoop (slightly less popular), or kicking a ball into a net (extraordinarily popular in places where a lot of coffee and drugs are grown). None of this entertains, and a good bit of it horrifies.

American football, which must command the attention of all straight men at all times, operates like a freak show. Young men, pumped up on steroids, human growth hormone, and 12,000-calorie-a-day diets gleefully blast each other into neurocognitive oblivion while fans pretend to be interested.

The fiction that these kids are natural athletes, as opposed to freakish examples of what can be achieved by a sports science cocktail, drives innumerable suburban kids into the clutches of the sports-science complex. The ghouls of the sports-science complex demand not just money from their charges, but their very childhoods.

In the United States, anyone who visits a gas station convenience store will be treated to the sight of a little cylindrical cup. This cup usually features the image of some smiling child who requires treatment for an unpronounceable ailment. This is how we fund children's hospitals. Meanwhile tuition and tax dollars provide an endless revenue stream for the creation of collegiate and professional stadiums, all for the development of sports that everyone secretly hates.

No one wants to spend four hours on a Saturday watching pretend student athletes, their faces covered in helmets, slam into one another while pursuing a small patch of real estate. This is why beer is involved. Nothing can be more joyless than an NCAA basketball game. These players, bred in countless Amateur Athletic Union (AAU) and other perpetual-play leagues, start every game with the full knowledge that their father-figure coach hopes to win only for the purpose of padding his resume so that he can move to a more lucrative scam at some larger school somewhere.

These players know this, just as well as they know that they could be driven off the squad in favor of some freshman with more fast-twitch muscle fibers. No hyphenated phrase can be more insincere than "student-athlete."

Women's sports are even more insincere. The WNBA may be the only organization of any kind built purely for reasons of political correctness. No one likes to watch women play basketball, and it is telling that no WNBA video game existed until 2017. Occasionally, someone will try to defend the WNBA on technical grounds with some comment like "since they don't have the same athletic ability as men, women have to play great technical basketball," which sounds just as insincere as a woman who claims that it doesn't matter if her boyfriend lacks in certain physical dimensions because it makes him develop superior lovemaking techniques. *Sure.*

Women don't even like to watch other women play sports. Women's tennis attracts male viewers only because it features long-limbed goddesses in short white skirts grunting, sweating, and tucking fuzzy balls up into their underwear. The Lingerie Football League (LFL) draws such large crowds that it renamed itself the Legends Football League to gain enough respectability to be featured on occasional cable broadcasts. The new title sounds less than sincere.

Pushed to its extreme, sports insincerity becomes professional wrestling. This is the irony behind World Wrestling Entertainment, which was formerly the World Wrestling Federation but changed to WWE after acquiring the National Wrestling Association, or NWA. The merger allowed each organization to not only make more money but to avoid the unfortunate association with the World Wildlife Federation and the 1980s rap group N-words With Attitude.

Pro wrestlers pretend to fight with one another, and this insincere conceit allows for the fight to become much more exciting than a real fight. Pro wrestlers flip through the air, press each other above their heads, and spat with each other like the members of an eighth-grade cheerleading squad. What does it mean to say that pro wrestling is "fake"? Fake in what sense? Is it fake because the practitioners are not really fighting to hurt one another? Pro wrestling, by owning up to its insincerity by furiously winking at its audience, actually is the sincerest sport in culture.

Pro wrestlers mug for the camera, perform entertaining stunts, and make everything personal. The immaculately fit women stuff their bodies into glowing halter tops and hot shorts, and bounce around in a ring while putting each other into "submission" holds (again, wink, wink) that have about as much to do with fighting as vibrating massagers have to do with relieving back pain. Meanwhile, the male wrestlers, fabulously shaved, tanned, and buff, preen and flex so much that it is hard to say the medium exploits female sexuality in any special way. The men are more naked than the women are.

Still, no one doubts that young men, particularly boys, make up the primary audience for professional wrestling. It may sound strange to say, but there's nothing overtly gay about the male performance in a pro-wrestling ring. The muscles are not for gay men to drool over (although one can imagine that this happens) but rather for young boys to admire. The hot chicks are for the dads to look at.

The WWE is vastly superior to most normal sports because the organization does not extort taxpayers to build vast and wasteful playgrounds, does not fund itself with tuition dollars, and does not concoct any justifications for itself. The only true insincerity from pro wrestling comes when the wrestlers themselves claim to have achieved their physiques without resorting to hormones and steroids, the untested abuse of which seems to have sent an abnormal number of them into early heart trauma and death.

The Ultimate Fighting Championships (UFC), in contrast, claims the tagline "As Real as It Gets." This makes no sense, of course, but neither does anything else about the UFC. Somehow—maybe it began when junior high and high schools became a legal obligation for everyone—most men carry an idea of what a "real" fight should be like. This vague definition usually involves two men squaring off in a somewhat open space without weapons. The fight ends when one person either submits or cannot continue due to severe injury or unconsciousness.

The Brazilians, denizens of a macho culture that evolved in the twentieth century turf wars involving surfing, created the concept of no-rules brawling through fights in dojos and on beaches. The famous Gracie family from Brazil created modern Mixed Martial Arts by developing a type of full-body jujitsu that used specialized takedowns and joint locks. For a long while, the Gracies issued a challenge to anybody who wanted to fight them, and they always won.

The Gracie family built the UFC in 1993 to showcase their jujitsu techniques in a public forum. In that first UFC, Royce Gracie, twenty-something and relatively slight of build, rolled through his opponents, thus proving the superiority of Brazilian jujitsu over all of the striking arts that emphasized punching and kicking. He did so in two subsequent UFCs, though not without challenges even as his brothers won victories in other organizations that showcased the same kind of no-rules fighting.

By televising their prowess, the Gracies ensured their own demise. Sure, they won every fight, but this was only because they knew what karate, kickboxing, and boxing were while their opponents had no idea what jujitsu was.

The Gracies developed specific techniques that allowed them to quickly take down punchers and kickers, while the opposite had yet to occur. Once the Brazilian jujitsu techniques got recorded on tape, fighters could prepare for them, and the insincere premise became revealed. The UFC eventually developed a rule set and gave fighters little gloves to wear and outlaws biting and eye-gouging, which would likely be the go-to acts in a "real" fight.

It was never clear what "real" fighting is to begin with. Can you use a lead pipe in a no-rules fight, and if not, then why? Is a real fight something that takes place in a parking lot or in a stairway? Can you enlist friends in your defense? Isn't war a real fight? Is it a real fight when the mafia orders that an informant be shot, unawares, in the back of the head? What does any of this mean?

History does record "rough-and-tumble" bouts in the American south where the combatants could bite and gouge. Apparently, that is so effective that when those activities are allowed, that's all that anyone does. What "as real as it gets" means does not matter because the UFC appeals to an illogical fan base made up of people who want to emulate the buffed and tattooed look of the fighters in the cage.

UFC fighters, promoters, and its defenders often say that fighting taps into something primal. Not really, no anthropologist has uncovered evidence of a human predilection for one-on-one fighting without weapons. Hunter-gatherer societies behave with a shocking level of day-to-day violence, but not in cages under prepared rules.

This notion of one-on-one fighting is a recent product that can be traced to boxing. Boxing, the modern form of which was born in eighteenth-century England, should be banned for its brutality, but everybody in boxing knows how filthy the "sport" is.

The fixed fight, still a feature of just about all boxing cards in one way or another, is the ultimate insincerity, but who can blame boxers for taking a payout? Between 2015 and 2017, three boxers in televised American fights took so many blows to the head that they had to have sections of their skulls removed so that their swelling brains would have somewhere to bulge. At least in boxing viewers will never be subjected to the sight of a man getting knocked out and then having his head bounced off the mat with several more punches, as frequently occurs in the cage.

The UFC, a repulsive public spectacle, pits fighters in a competition only to uphold the insincere facade of sport. People watch because they want to see another human being suffer from debilitating head trauma. Watching another individual suffer from sudden and catastrophic brain damage satisfies the human criteria for both humor and fear. Concussions cause people to jerk and fall in funny ways, to twitch unexpectedly.

One cannot hope, publicly, to see this happen to children or the elderly, but when it happens to well-muscled male athletes the spectacle becomes acceptable, and the fact that the combatants have the opportunity to defend themselves lends an insincere moral cover to the whole disgusting process.

Here is what the UFC is: disgusting, immoral, money-grubbing, and degenerative to society. Here is what the UFC is not: dominated by wizened

Chinese Tai-Chi masters who have memorized Taoist aphorisms. This point may seem obvious, but for all of its insincerity the UFC did manage to expose the concept of the Chinese Kung Fu master as ass-kicking sensation to be a total fraud.

The kind of martial arts taught in Shaolin temples and American strip malls has more in common with country line dancing than it does actual fighting. The most insincere character of Asian stereotypes is the old martial arts master, armed with nothing but the power of suggestion, a wimp claiming to be the most powerful warrior in the world but unable to show it because of a secret honor code.

Something similar exists in Indian history, although the concept of the wise man is divorced from punching and kicking. R. K. Narayan's comic classic *The Guide* stars a protagonist named Raju as a beggar who gets mistaken for a holy man. As a holy man he "soon realized that his spiritual status would be enhanced if he grew a beard and long hair fell to his nape. A clean-shaven, close-haired saint was an anomaly" (2006 [1958], 39). Consider this brilliant passage:

> I came to be called Railway Raju. Perfect strangers, having heard of my name, began to ask for me when their train arrived at the Malgudi railway station. It is written on the brow of some that they shall not be left alone. I am one such, I think. Although I never looked for acquaintances, they somehow came looking for me. Men who had just arrived always stopped at my shop for a soda or cigarettes and to go through the book stack, and almost always they asked, "how far is . . . ?" or "Which way does one go to reach . . . ?" or "Are there many historical spots here?" or "I heard that your River Sarayu has its source somewhere on those hills and that it is a beauty spot." This sort of inquiry soon led me to think that I had not given sufficient thought to the subject. I never said "I don't know." Not in my nature, I suppose. If I had the inclination to say "I don't know what you are talking about," my life would have taken a different turn. Instead, I said, "Oh, yes, a fascinating place. Haven't you seen it? You must find the time to visit it, otherwise your whole trip here would be a waste." I am sorry I said it, an utter piece of falsehood. It was not because I wanted to utter a falsehood, but only because I wanted to be pleasant. (2006 [1958], 41)

If you don't know the answer to something, then say something nebulous and make sure you have long hair and a beard. The masses will fancy you a prophet, particularly if you live in a place that white people consider to be exotic.

Wise men serve no purpose, other than to talk vaguely, and sports only exist to give people something to talk about specifically. Only a select few fans actually find emotional connection to a collegiate or professional team, and one wonders whether this is healthy for them. In the late 1990s and early 2000s, the NASCAR racing association suckered hillbillies out of more money than Kentucky Fried Chicken by pretending that having a bunch of guys with greasy fingers and mid-1980s haircuts drive around in a circle was a sport. Nobody bought it, but country folk everywhere pretended to like the sport because it gave them something safe to watch and talk about while talking on the CB or getting drunk.

The insincerity of NASCAR involved creating a platform where people like Richard Petty or Dale Earnhardt could reap some fame. Dale, in particular, looked and sounded like any average redneck who ran a work crew. His mustache and heavy shades could be easily replicated by anybody who wanted to drive the back roads and see a little bit of Dale staring back at them from the rearview mirror. Romantically, Dale died on the race track "doing what he loved," everyone reminded each other repeatedly, which makes a thinking person wonder if Dale really loved getting his neck broken in a car crash.

Insincerity killed NASCAR because, by posing as a real sport, race car drivers from foreign countries have been encouraged to start competing, and NASCAR's hillbilly base, which really only wanted to have an excuse to drink moonshine with other hill people, cannot identify with mincing Europeans who now drive around in circles on Sunday afternoons.

As a side note, Will Ferrell's 2006 film *Talladega Nights: The Ballad of Ricky Bobby* may never be shown on Turner Classics, but Bobby's rivalry with a gay European driver does capture the evolution of NASCAR into ratings oblivion. It also showed that NASCAR fans can take a joke pretty well.

That movie brings up another point about heterosexual aggression against homosexuals: there is no counterexample. One does not encounter in society or literature a raging gay man who just wants to stomp straight people. Nor does an aggressive anti-straight linguistic culture like that exist among homosexual men.

Again, the purpose of "faggot" jokes or aggressive gay impressions (lisping, flouncing, and the like) may appear to be intended to insult homosexuals, but the unstated purpose really is to create a bond between heterosexual men and to ensure that others get the point that the person telling the gay joke really prefers sexual congress with women.

This is another reason why straight men find it perplexing when people outside of that circle see all the offensiveness but none of the humor, which reiterates that the purpose of those kinds of jokes really is to determine who gets to be in the inner hetero-circle.

Women may or may not have this problem. Females seem a lot less concerned about lesbianism than men have traditionally been about male gayness. Is this because lesbianism, with the kittenish licks and soft clitoral touches seems less offensive to everyone? Everybody likes lesbians; or at least the concept of lesbian sex. For years, before girl-on-girl action became not only accepted but celebrated (a prevalent rumor is out that there may be some scenes involving lesbian sex somewhere on the Internet), many lesbians went out of their way to look as butch and unattractive as possible.

You know the look: short hair, sleeveless shirt, shoulder tattoos, no makeup, wallet with a chain, a look of vague dissatisfaction with the thought that penises might be somewhere in the vicinity. How insincere! What connects lesbian sex with looking like a dockworker or part-time rodeo cowboy?

By co-opting the look of men, lesbians simply played further into the power structure—like a black woman dying her hair blonde and wearing blue contact lenses. The genius of the butch lesbians, however, was that they took all of the sexuality out of their sexuality. By appearing as an unattractive as possible, they removed their sexual orientation from the fantasies of men and claimed it for their own.

It did not work, of course, because the market dictates too much. Hot chicks making out will always find an audience because the conceit attracts male attention. Straight men could be standing anywhere in the world, on some sun-soaked mountainous vista in New Zealand, or overlooking the rolling green hills of Ireland, and if some attractive lass in a tight pair of cut-off jeans and a tube top walked by, every head would turn.

Markets get this. "Breastaurants" like Hooters or Twin Peaks make a joke of their insincerity. The Hooters logo is an owl. The Twin Peaks logo is a pair of mountains. This provides the smallest veneer of culpable deniability. Men used to buy *Playboy* for the articles; now they go to Hooters for the wings.

Playboy used to actually publish decent fiction and journalism, something that seems almost respectable in an era where women on the Internet's most popular sites must act insincere indeed if they are to look as if they are enjoying whatever the hell is being done to or on their orifices. The food at these breastaurants tastes like rat meat roasted for eight minutes over a candle, but the view is (presumably) nice, at least it is if one is turned on by the sight of single moms' enduring humiliation. Seeing women in their proper place as sexual objects and food servers might be the real point of these places.

Before venturing into the romantics and their emphasis on sincerity; let's begin with the fact that Mary Wollstonecraft (1759–1797) recognized that male philosophers rarely did women any good. In her *A Vindication of the Rights of Woman*, she wrote "I may be accused of arrogance; still I must declare what I firmly believe, that all the writers who have written on the subject of female education and manners from Rousseau to Dr. Gregory, have contributed to render women more artificial, weak characters than they otherwise would have been" (2006 [1792], 31).

Rousseau's condescension brewed up Wollstonecraft's frustration; misunderstandings about women should not feature in grand philosophical statements. She saw these philosophies as insincere, "As a philosopher, I read with indignation the plausible epithets which men use to soften their insults; and, as a moralist, I ask what is meant by such heterogenous associations, as fair defects, amiable weaknesses etc." (2006 [1792], 46). Wollstonecraft simply got sick of her sex being praised into powerlessness; insincere condescension perfumed with poetic words stank worse than outright and sincere oppression.

This brings up the point that sincerity itself can even be insincere. When Jean Jacques Rousseau wrote "Man is born free, yet everywhere is in chains" in 1762, he wrote under the assumption that civilization itself corrupted humanity from a previously pristine state. Enlightenment philosophers, in these days before anthropology, argued a good bit over the natural state of man because the nature of humanity provided a good starting point for arguments about the role of civilization.

We might call the Enlightenment the era of the philosophical anthropologist. The Enlightenment philosophers seemed to hold little truck with the Old Testament story about the creation of humankind but, rather, imagined humans in a "state of nature" that supposedly said something about the true nature of man and, therefore, of society.

Christianity taught that from the time of inception, each human being possessed a sinful nature. As children of Adam and Eve, humans escaped the birth canal into a carnal world of sin where they fit perfectly. Only by engaging in "good works" as defined by Catholic doctrine, could humans become redeemed. Catholics confessed, prayed, paid alms, and said last rites all in an attempt to alter their true nature so that heaven might be attained.

Luther and the Protestants agreed about the sin nature of humans; all the hubbub known as the Protestant Reformation came about as a result of a disagreement about how salvation could be achieved. Luther thought good works to be useless as a means to salvation; only faith alone in the redeeming power of Jesus's blood sacrifice could earn entrance into heaven. Luther believed that the mother church provided an insincere facade rather than sincere salvation.

In his book *The Leviathan*, Thomas Hobbes (1588–1679), who lived through the English Civil Wars (1642–1651) and saw just how deeply the reaper's scythe could cut with politics on one edge and religion on the other, agreed that humans came out of the womb in an evil state. Hobbes saw the nastiness of the seventeenth century as revealing the true nature of humanity.

Rather than corrupting human nature, civilization revealed and extended it. Politics and religions were extrapolations of human nature, not the corruptions that came with civilized morals. Far from a monolithic monster, the Leviathan consisted of untold numbers of wriggling little worms of hatred inside of every person. Only when combined did the worms create a single amorphous beast.

Only the powerful state, a larger beast, could control the worm population. Human nature, inherently evil, had to be kept in check. Absent authority, human beings only behave themselves because they can be certain that everyone else is just as bad. The inherent threat of retaliation holds back one's nature in society when the state proves incapable of doing so.

In his "An Essay Concerning Human Understanding" (1689), John Locke thought that humans escaped the birth canal in an inherently empty state; neither good nor bad, but empty of morals and thoughts. Experience gave humans their personalities; they carried no ancient trace of sin but could not be described as good either.

Psychology, the goal of which might be described as the individual's attempt to be sincere with him or herself, derives from this insight as does sociology. Locke's premise makes demands on society; the thinking is that a perfect society could produce perfect people. The messiness of human interactions makes it difficult for books and theories to control people; open violence works better.

With his rousing first line, Rousseau announced—with the fresh-faced enthusiasm of one who has never read a history book or seen someone of a different faith or religious persuasion impaled on a pike or burned at the stake—that human nature was free, happy, and ultimately good. This meant that the miserable state of humanity could be attributed to the corrupting effects of society. Civilization, by forcing wild and passionate humans to act civilized, greedy, and unemotional, created insincerity and, therefore, misery.

All of Rousseau's insights into the state of human nature came into being at the same time that the Industrial Revolution and the British Parliament tore up the deeply entangled roots of agrarian civilization through technological innovation and the Enclosure Acts (begun in 1604). The latter law allowed for Parliament to essentially steal what had once been public lands for the purpose of handing it over to industrialists. In a double win for capitalism (which never has much trouble winning), the industrialists gained territory for factories while the newly land-less peasantry had no choice but to hand themselves over for meager wages in the newly developed factories.

A screw-the-people scheme of that magnitude required a bit of ideological cover, and the government soon got it. Theorists who claimed that industrialization and all the misery it brought were simply natural forms of economic evolution vomited up chunky strings of words. From all of this came sooty cities, long hours, barely hid prostitution, and the development of a new kind of Western civilization. Insincerity reigned in this new environment.

Rousseau's work links the Enlightenment to the romantics. The factories poisoned the air even as the nobility fashioned new ideologies to justify their theft of land and personal freedom. To avoid the cities, one must return to the country to see it with fresh eyes. Purification came in the water breaking across the seaside crags, and poetry flowed in the streams. The countryside provided just the right antidote for the city, and sincere emotion could save humanity from the assembly lines and long hours. Boredom could be healed with poems. For the romantics, insincerity posed the greatest danger to the human condition.

The romantics focused not only on love between men and women but also on love for children. As romantic royalty, Rousseau sought to banish insincerity entirely from his fantasy kingdom. He wrote the novel *Emile*, which encouraged parents to let their children run wild in a state of nature for as long as possible before corrupting them with civilized things such as books and reading.

In *The Confessions*, Rousseau subjects his audience to every tedious and sordid detail of his life. The point of the work was that he could objectively look at his own life without any insincere self-aggrandizement or apology. The age of candor began, and the first great work of psychological self-study, Freud before Freud, was also the last. Thanks, Rousseau, for inventing the tiresome genre of the personal memoir, which might be described as a not-quite novel for people not quite talented enough to write a novel.

A personal monster, Rousseau repeatedly knocked up a servant wench but then dropped the inconvenient babies off at one of the rat-infested orphanages that seemed to blight the cities of Europe at that time. His passion for life and children only extended to theoretical beings. This brings up an interesting question: Can one be insincere in the pursuit of sincerity? In other words, by trying to outdo each other in their sincere appreciation of not just nature but of the rhyming words that described it, did the romantics go too far? Did the abyss also stare into them?

At some point, everybody just got sick of all that weepiness not long after von Goethe published *The Sorrows of Young Werther* in 1774, which may be the great ode to sincerity. Mercifully small, the book may not translate well into English but it's not clear how "My whole heart was full at that moment; the recollection of various events in the past pressed upon my soul, and tears came to my eyes" would sound acceptable in any language (von Goethe 1989 [1774], 49).

Too many tears diluted the sincerity, and anyone who cares to research the lives of Lord Byron or Percy Bysshe Shelley finds too little to admire. Young and sexy they may have been, but maybe that was the problem. Shelley could never discern between the music of his muses and his sirens, and he died on the sea, too early to make amends for the transgressions of his youth.

Only his wife, Mary, lived on to publish the great Gothic tale about a man possessed by too much scientific power. For Mary, who lived only a few days as an infant by her mother's side, who would bury a child and a husband before she turned twenty, a fascination with reversing death surely came sincerely through her pen.

The romantics later faced a realist backlash, but damn the realists for that. What could be a more beautiful philosophy for the young than romanticism? What replaced it? For young women of intelligence, surely a man who writes doggerel and enjoys a hike by the seaside is still superior to those who turn their baseball caps backward and game online. Bring back the poets and the hikers who take the time to swoon at a potential love interest and banish the social media hookup, so many of which supposedly begin with the insincere phrase "Netflix and chill?"

Even romantics must admit that this "love at first sight" business seems insincere, if not dangerous. Shakespeare invented it with *Romeo and Juliet*, and although the concept became a feature of Western civilization and literature, Shakespeare likely invented it as a way of getting an important plot point out of the way.

Romeo looks at Juliet while at a costume party and instantly falls in love. She reciprocates, and Romeo can get on with the sword fights. What is brilliant for a play can take on the overtones of stalking in real life, but perhaps the whole notion of love at first sight is a code for the romantics. One has to believe in it for it to happen, and when the young fail to attend the theater, perhaps they fail to give themselves a chance to shape a pleasant insincerity.

The romantics bestowed upon Western civilization the archetype of the alienated genius, the sensitive soul who seeks solitude in the rough patches of the world. Surrounded by nature, books, and thoughts, the romantic genius could then point out the flaws of civilization. Self-knowledge, enhanced through the reading and creation of literature, could change an otherwise broken society.

Politics ruined it, as it always does. Soon enough, political violence as a force of change became a romantic staple, and discussions soon turned to the concept of individual freedoms and the nature of the relationship between citizens and the government. Thomas Jefferson, and by proxy all the other white males associated with the foundation of the United States of America, get accused of hypocrisy all the time by people who have read half a history book once.

Calling Jefferson a hypocrite is ahistorical. He might have been insincere, but not hypocritical when he wrote "We hold these truths to be self-evident, that all men are created equal." This is where the sages always point out that Jefferson really meant that all *white* men are created equal. The hypocrisy of the founders makes this statement insincere because the stated purpose and the real purpose of the phrase fail to match up.

Not true. The Declaration's primary intended audience consisted of one person, King George III. A limited monarch he may have been, and a German on top of that, but King George derived whatever powers that Parliament had not taken in 1688 through the Divine Right of Kings. This meant he believed himself to be unequal.

Jefferson's Declaration reads like a revolutionary syllogism with the first phrase acting as a geometric axiom. The Declaration's philosophy is like one of Da Vinci's mirror scripts; it can only be read when held up to its reflection, which is the Divine Right of Kings. That simple bit of doctrine declared that kings get their power to rule from God, and that this makes the people "subjects." Flip it upside down so that the people get their rights from God and then create governments to protect those rights, and you get the idea. Conservatives tend to fall back on the Declaration because, having scoured the Constitution and finding neither the word *God* or the word of God, they hope to grasp for a Christian founding in the written words of a man who wavered between agnosticism and a watery deism. Talk about insincere.

After the romantics, the notion of the alienated genius continued to antagonize Western civilization. People of true artistic or philosophical talent strive to be recognized for talent; there's really no other purpose for producing art but the desire to maintain the image of a tortured soul. The perpetuation of this notion is aided by the fact that geniuses like this do occasionally surface and produce something worth noticing.

The Russian mathematician Grigori Perelman (b. 1966), for example, proved the Poincaré conjecture after a decade of working nearly alone in his frozen apartment. He shared his work only with the mathematical community and did so just enough to explain to others the specifics of his solution. He won a one-million-dollar millennial prize for his work but refused the money. When he won the Fields Medal, he refused that, too.

Perelman really wanted to just do the math, which brings up an earlier question: "What's so great about sincerity?" For sincerity's sake, Perelman sits freezing in a Russian apartment when he could be drinking piña coladas on the Riviera with some of that big math genius money. This may be why sincerity enjoys a better reputation than insincerity; no one can do anything truly great without a sincere interest in the topic.

Perelman deserves to be considered a genius, and his refusal of the worldly things thrown his way reflects what is likely a genuine perplexity that he likely has toward the world. What, exactly, is the connection between deriving complex mathematical principles and spending money?

True artists should never seek accolades, and this creates a problem. Philosophers and artists once served at the court of the powerful as advisors or as exemplars of the state's power of patronage, but the romantic archetype encouraged philosophers and artists to separate themselves from society in search of great truths. This happened just as a free market formed. Being misunderstood might be ego satisfying, but being understood helps keep the landlord at bay.

Nietzsche and Marx, the architects eventually of eighteenth-century rightist and leftist politics, both worked largely in isolation but partially within the university institutions they both badly needed for intellectual stimulation and credibility. Neither sold well. Marx married and had children, and he needed the patronage of Engels to keep out of full penury; even then the Marx family suffered from abject poverty.

Philosophers with a self-concept of an alienated genius cannot simply take a job, so Marx scribbled and dreamed that the growling coming from the bellies of his children really came from the throats of an angry proletariat. Nietzsche never impregnated anyone that we know of and found it all the easier to be dreamy because of it.

The most alienated character in American literature goes by the name of Holden Caulfield, a prep-school teenager whose hatred for the insincerity he sees in the social climbers around him drives him eventually into a psychiatric home. *The Catcher in the Rye* (1951) amounts to great American literature; don't let anyone ever tell you any differently, but it baits critics because it's a book that captures a particular time in a person's life and embodies the raw emotions of adolescence.

Critics might point out that Caulfield whines too much, that his caustic and cynical schtick becomes tedious. This may be true, but Caulfield believes in the power of sincerity and finds that avoiding phonydom amounts to avoiding society; hence his eventual committal.

In *Anti-Oedipus* (1972), the French psychologists Gilles Deleuze and Félix Guattari argued that schizophrenia is a perfectly rational response to an irrational society. In other words, when society presents symptoms of insanity, then a sane person will be described and treated as the opposite. Sincerity in an insincere society poses as insanity.

The Catcher in the Rye reflects this concept through literature, and Caulfield speaks with an emotional rawness that endears him to readers who are either in the throes of adolescence or who can remember that time. All of us come into the world ignorant of the rules by which it works.

For just a few years of blissful innocence, it is possible for a select few to find to comfort in the arms of parents, grandparents, and the insincere myths of childhood—fairies and elves and such and such—but then some event brings about the grand "what the hell?" moment when all that gets ripped away and we realize that the spinning blue ball we all stand on contains hazards.

A grandparent or uncle dies and gets put underground, or Mom and Dad separate, or a baseball hits the mouth, and then the child understands the concept of pain and death but only emotionally and not cognitively. It sticks in the background and festers into anxiety. Adolescence is the period where the intellect fetches those anxiety-producing moments out of the background and connects them to reality.

These new realizations correspond with an influx of sexual hormones, and the all-too-often belief in the phoniness of the world finds expression in sexual rebellion. Or, for boys like Holden, the donning of a red hunting cap speaks to a sense of individuality and sincerity in a society that rewards insincerity. Adolescence is the only time when a person can get away with such clownish sincerity.

Recent biographies of Salinger himself, the most reclusive of writers, undress him publicly as a fraud. He carefully calibrated a public image of himself as a lone genius, and used that as a lure to keep public attention on him. Had Salinger lived long enough, he might have created a Twitter feed in his name merely for the purpose of never posting anything.

In the 1990s, grunge bands attempted the same trick. Pearl Jam achieved the heights of rock fame by pretending to not want any publicity. However, as Kim Neely wrote in her book about lead singer Eddie Vedder and the band, "Even if Eddie was as tortured by Pearl Jam's celebrity as he claimed to be, his insistence on using every interview to drive that home often made him seem more calculated—even self-aggrandizing—than candid" (1998, 254).

In the modern era, disaffected writers only get noticed when they massacre people in significant enough numbers to attract news trucks. Then, whatever blog entry the killer entered last gets upgraded to a "manifesto." Peaceful manifesto writers surely cringe whenever this happens, as it degrades the public perception of what a well-written manifesto should look like, and then further perpetuates the impression that all manifesto writers must be planning to massacre people in the name of a cause.

Nothing destroys young souls like finding out that the tortured artist who despises insincerity is, himself, insincere. Perhaps the healthy way to deal with insincerity is simply to theorize its impact on all of society. Erving Goffman did just this in his book *The Presentation of Self in Everyday Life*, which is the original classic on the topic of insincerity. Goffman sticks with a single metaphor: we are all actors on different stages and correlates the "backstage" with a person's sincerer self. In the introduction, he wrote:

> I assume that when an individual appears before others he will have many motives for trying to control the impression they receive of the situation. This report is concerned with some of the common techniques that persons employ to sustain such impressions and with some of the common contingencies associated with the employment of these techniques. The specific content of any activity presented by the individual participant, or the role it plays in the interdependent activities of an on-going social system, will not be at issue; I shall be concerned only with the participant's dramaturgical problems of presenting the activity before others. (1959, 15)

According to Goffman, waiters and waitresses act a certain way "backstage" but put on an actor's face when on-stage in front of customers. All "professionals" must maintain their insincere faces at all times or face the injury of being unprofessional. To sling a high kick at someone's head, or growl a slur at some office backstabber is to risk being fired, prosecuted, and ruined entirely. In too great of a dose, insincerity can be poison. In small doses, it is medicinal.

Students of literature and psychology might be interested in the way that novels depict insincerity. *Pride and Prejudice* (1813), for example, features a sincere woman who believes that her suitor is insincere, only to discover he is not. Romance ensues. This poses a question: Does romance depend upon insincerity? What role does passive-aggressive behavior, which by definition is aggressiveness masked as passivity, play in interactions among equals? How, exactly, should one feel when treated insincerely by a peer?

KEY POINTS

- Each person wants to impress an image of him or herself on society, and when other people refuse to reflect the right image, the result is frustration. Only in cases of extreme emotion or accomplishment do other people agree to act the way we want them to, such is the case at weddings, funerals, and award ceremonies.
- Sports exist for purposes other than entertainment, mostly to give straight men an excuse to engage socially with each other while they pretend they are interested in athletic activities.
- Shakespeare probably made up love at first sight in *Romeo and Juliet* just to get an important plot point out of the way without boring the audience—but the idea is not bad, and the play is great.
- Entertainments that employ comedy or horror must use an insincere setup to elicit a response from the audience; true humor and horror exists spontaneously and sincerely "in the wild."
- The romantics and the Enlightenment philosophers praised sincerity and emotion, but Mary Wollstonecraft saw the insincerity in this in that the poetry tended to turn women into objects of affection only.
- Erving Goffman thought that insincerity was so crucial to sociological studies that he wrote a book around the analogy of humans being like stage actors.
- Alienated geniuses are supposed to be sincere, but, all too often, the facade of the alienated genius hides a cynical artist manipulating his image.
- Curse words and scatological humor are ways to gauge the status of a relationship. People only curse or tell dirty jokes with their societal equals.

Chapter Four

Insincerity in Society and with the Self

Reputable news websites occasionally report on celebrity sex scandals using a peculiar double entendre. Some hacker, usually one of these heavily breasted males with crème cookies stuffed in the pocket of his ironic T-shirt, sneaks into the cell phone of a celebrity gal and steals images and/or video of her engaged in acts of vicarious sexuality. When this makes its way to the darker sites of the Internet, new sources report the stealing of the sexual tape as if it was news. Then, just to stir in a little more sugar, these sites tend to give details as to the actual specifics of the sexual acts.

This brings up an ethical question: If we consider the attainment of sexual videos and pictures through thievery to be a crime, and we do, then why is the reporting of the theft not a furtherance of the crime? The thief committed the act of stealing, but the real crime lies in the public humiliation of a starlet, athlete, or model. To perpetuate that humiliation by reporting on what was on the ill-gotten tapes makes an organization accomplice to the crime.

Yet, who can blame the news media for reporting the kind of news that people want to read? If readers then click on the incognito tab on their phones and then find the stolen pornography on some First Amendment protected celebrity pornography site, then so be it. Would they be so quick to do so if their own viewing habits then duly became reported? The news helps us lie to ourselves.

Something similar occurred when a website for adulterers, Ashley Madison, got hacked in 2015. Men who opted onto this site found themselves robo-messaged but rarely ever met any women actually on the prowl for a purely sexual affair. Grown men should know that anything that advertises itself as being about satisfying male sexuality must be an insincere scam.

Collegiate spring break, for example, usually attracts nothing but young bozos. They all find themselves either drinking from red Dixie cups while they futilely try to pull one of the few young fawns away from her protective group, or else find themselves watching a tired thirty-something local get water drenched on her white T-shirt for the nineteenth consecutive year.

In fact, it is hard to conceive that any of the millions of men on Ashley Madison ever got anywhere near a real woman for sexual purposes. The whole concept of adultery might be entirely overblown in society, kept alive for insincere reasons of titillation and fantasy. Where, exactly, do people find the time for these things? It happens just enough for people to think it happens all the time.

Still, it's hard to imagine something more fully insincere than Ashley Madison. The site itself dripped insincerity as it advertised adultery that it could not deliver. There's an excellent chance that most of the men who signed up for the site did so merely out of curiosity; they wanted to see what kind of gals hid behind the veil. Yet, when the site got hacked and the names of Ashley Madison's customers revealed, the public reacted as if all the men on the site possessed some deep moral failing. This sanctimony, too, seems a bit insincere, but who knows?

Back in the early 2000s, the television journalist Chris Hansen entered into full-scale popular consciousness with his Dateline *To Catch a Predator* bit about baiting grown men into thinking they were coming to a home to hook up sexually with a teenage girl. It made for great, if highly disturbing, television. Unsuspecting men would show up to a girl's house after a period of online chatting, and then Hansen would walk out and shame them.

Like all forms of shaming pornography, *To Catch a Predator* shocked at first, and audience members could claim, somewhat credibly, that the show possessed the redeeming feature of being a warning about the dangers of online chatting. Hansen made a nice little ratings grab with this gimmick, and kept on throwing out more and more lines into the waters, hoping to catch more predators. Subsequent shows brought in new features; an actual teenage girl could be heard and sometimes seen as a way of baiting the men into the house. Sometimes, a fake teenaged boy got dangled from the online lure.

Soon, police became a feature, and they sometimes came in four at a time to wrestle some unsuspecting would-be criminal with a double chin and blue jean shorts from Walmart to the ground. More and more, however, the predators came in with dark skin and foreign accents. These were simply impoverished men from foreign countries; American women probably did not find them desirable, and their home cultures might not have had taboos on relationships with girls that American law would consider to be under the age of consent.

At some point, the whole conceit reeked with insincerity. Hansen, who started off as appearing as a social-justice warrior, looked sleazier with every gotcha moment. By the second or third episode, many of the men ceased to look surprised so much as undone by their own naivety. They "knew it!"

many of them shouted as they pulled shirts up over their faces. Knew what? Knew that real sex had never been on offer, only a ruse followed by humiliation and a lifetime's worth of being registered as a sexual offender?

On the surface, *To Catch a Predator* looks a bit like MTV's many prank-based shows. The pranked person walks in expecting one kind of situation and instead gets another; in this case, the humor came from seeing someone walking in expecting to have illegal sex, but instead finding himself humiliated by the very desire that brought him there in the first place.

All too often, with the bright lights on them, the predators would claim that they never intended to really statutorily rape anyone. They had come to protect the girl, out of boredom, just to see if it was real. One man, a foreigner, got pranked so well that he stripped naked, and when Hansen walked in he barked at the man to put on a towel before he sat down for his interrogation. The man's nudity would seem to rob him of any plausible deniability, but guilt may not be so assured for the others.

How do we discern the level of the crime from Ashley Madison to *To Catch a Predator*? Is one more culpable for chatting online with a robot claiming to be a fake married woman or for chatting online with police or reporters who claim to be fake teenage girls? Does showing up at the house indicate a greater level of intent than chatting online? Where do we determine that a perpetrator crossed the line from intent to action?

Is it sincere to feel badly for the men when the bright lights come on and the police slam them to the floor? To claim that such a feeling is tantamount to approving of statutory rape would be insincere; that notion only provides justification for the glorious feeling of watching other people in the throes of humiliation. Would a show that humiliates rich sexual tourists in Haiti or Thailand grab the same level of ratings?

The nausea-inducing thing about *To Catch a Predator* really doesn't involve the premise. Surely, it's no secret that some percentage of the population will eagerly grab at illicit and illegal sex. However, the singular purpose of the shows is to horrify the audience while also allowing it a feeling of superiority.

Insincerity in society cannot be separate from insincerity with the self, as the difference between the public and private self cannot really be defined. The men on Ashley Madison, as well as those hapless losers who walked into Chris Hansen's shame trap, likely contained a dual consciousness that allowed each of them to deny what they were doing right up to that point.

In other words, they might have been generating an arena where something unethical could occur, but kept themselves convinced that they could control the situation and leave it. When the situation suddenly controlled them, they found that their private mental justifications looked dull in the television lights.

To return to an earlier notion, the reason that resistance against a true totalitarian state really is futile has to do with the fact that everyone in a state really looks out for him or herself. When totalitarian regimes lighten up just enough so that dissenters no longer get locked up, tortured, and/or executed, this allows for enough protests to arise so that it appears the balance of power might shift.

Today's revolutionaries might be tomorrow's bosses; and most people wait to see what might happen before placing a wager either for or against. Holding themselves in a dual-state allows people to say that they were either "always for" or "always against" the revolution depending on how it turned out.

Do we all do this? Do we all hold our emotions and opinions in a kind of Schrodinger's Cat state until things turn out one way or another, at which point we insincerely proclaim our "real" position? One of the great questions to come out of the twentieth century was this: Can we have a self that is separate from our actions? Is it the case that a person can act in such a way that is "not him" while under coercion?

The Nuremberg Trials judged that Nazis who stated "I was just following orders" did not possess a sufficient defense. By doing this, the Nuremberg court gave backing to the Protestant concept of individual judgment, a moral concept stating that, no matter the circumstances, you, and no one else, must control your own actions.

Using Hitler and/or the Nazis as an analogy or comparison may be the worst political cliché, but the fact that it occurs so often indicates just how deeply the Nazi era imprinted upon social conscience and morals. After World War I, writers, poets, and musicians developed an entire antiwar, and therefore antiauthority, literature that painted "patriots" as saps and governments as vile and brutal. Nazism's rise shunted these sentiments to the side in Germany, but a lack of will to fight in yet another government-led debacle surely contributed to France's rapid defeat in the Second World War.

The Nuremberg judgment empowered individuals to resist any Western governments' drive to war. All of a sudden, individuals who sincerely wanted to avoid fighting could express this and expect some legal backing, particularly in Europe. After all, if you individually can be held responsible after the war for your actions during the war, this gives you some control over whether you take orders. Insincerity, in other words, cannot be used as a defense, and this opened the way for sincere resistance.

In 1993, Disney produced a melodrama titled *Swing Kids*, about a group of teenagers in 1939 Hamburg, Germany, who engaged in a mild rebellion against the local Nazi Party. The Nazis, and their youth group Hitlerjugend (referred to as HJ throughout the film), disapprove of swing dancing and its American-Jewish-Negro origins.

The movie lacks artistic merit but does feature a young Robert Sean Leonard as Peter. Leonard never managed to cure himself of overacting until he reached his role as the oncologist Wilson on *House*, and his screams and tears only add off-key howls to a bad script.

Thomas, Peter's best friend, is played by a young Christian Bale. Barbara Hershey plays Peter's mother, and Kenneth Branagh a creepy Nazi bureaucrat. Everyone speaks English, but Hershey's character and some of the bad guys speak with a German accent while the teenagers all speak like American high-schoolers.

The plot involves the swing kids stumbling into situations that require actions; Peter, the main character, confronts Hitler Youths beating up a Jewish boy and has to rescue his mother from a Nazi block leader who smacks her face while trying to talk her into trying prostitution. It goes on like this, with one contrived scene after another, until Peter and Thomas get in trouble for stealing a radio (only from the Nazis, though, and for a good cause) and then Peter gets forced into joining the HJ. Thomas then joins as well and declares that he and Peter can be "HJ by day, swing kids by night."

The screenwriters for this mess of a movie, through no fault of their own, pinpointed a crucial element regarding insincerity in society. Peter and Thomas make a pact to be insincere but find that they cannot do so. Thomas embraces Nazism and Peter finally rejects it. The screenwriters could not have intended to make a statement about insincerity because the movie tries to redeem Thomas at the end, and the director cannot keep a sense of continuity from one screen shot to the next (Peter's defiant brother picks up an umbrella that is nowhere to be seen in the previous sequence), but a message comes out nonetheless.

All the people in the film who stand up to the Nazis get either carted off to prison or commit suicide. The fate of the fourth swing kid—who never takes a stand either way and disappears entirely about halfway through the movie once his purpose of providing a fourth swing kid seems to have been served—remains a great cinematic mystery.

Most people don't take a stand either way on anything. They hold alternative beliefs in their head and then choose a side after it's clear who is going to win. This leads to questions in general about insincerity with the self and the concept of what Harvard professor and philosopher Fiery Cushman calls "moral luck." Moral luck has to do with the way that an action can be defined depending upon its outcome, which Cushman actually sees as philosophically unjustifiable. To illustrate the point, he explained the concept to David Edmonds and Nigel Warburton for a *Philosophy Bites* book:

> Imagine that, after this interview, you and I went out for a couple of beers. Then each of us got into our separate cars to go home. On your way home, you fall asleep at the wheel and you run off the road and run into a pile of bushes

and get picked up for drunk driving. . . . I don't know about the laws in Britain, but in my home state of Massachusetts you could expect to receive a $250 fine.

On my way home, I fall asleep and I run off the road and I hit a person and kill him. In Massachusetts, I could expect 2.5 to 15 years in prison. Those are radically different amounts of punishment for what amounts to identical behavior. The twentieth-century British philosopher, Bernard Williams, pointed out that in this respect morality seems to depend on luck. (2014, 134–35)

By this philosophy, those of us who walk around thinking of ourselves as relatively good people really might be the moral equivalent of someone who committed vehicular manslaughter. Are we all insincere with ourselves? Ever imbibe a few, make it home, and then wake up the next day thinking of yourself as basically a good human being who did something risky and stupid? Or, if not, ever do something equivalent? Is it the case that every incident of texting and driving that does not cause a vehicular death equates to vehicular manslaughter?

Are we all insincere in our self-concepts? Is our self-respect based insincerely around the fact that we, as decent human beings, have been morally lucky? Dr. Cushman's "moral luck" philosophy contains a few significant problems that actually connect to other forms of insincerity within the self.

All of us regret actions we have taken, and all of us probably wonder "what would have happened" had we taken a different path in life—chosen a different career, chosen to get married or not get married, gotten vanilla rather than chocolate. Yet, fantasizing about a different life path makes no sense in terms of physics and statistics.

Consider this: the people you see in the newspaper who get hit by cars while riding ten speeds, or the friends you know on social media who just got a surprise divorce; they are all living out the consequences of decisions made in the past. If we think of those as "alternative pathways" from another lifetime, then we can see the problem with any "I should have done that" concept.

Let's imagine a happily married newspaper writer who wishes that she had studied electrical engineering in college instead of journalism; does she consider that this might have caused her to go to the library late one night where she might have met a different person and then entered into what would become a failed marriage?

The point is that wondering what might have happened if you took a different path in life amounts to pointless revolving speculation. Obviously, someone sitting in a prison cell for committing a serious crime might consider that other life choices would probably have led to better outcomes, but as a general rule, the unpredictability of cause and effect chains makes any question about regret really pointless. No alternative paths exist, only odds about what might occur and without any "reality" to check those against, they remain statistical possibilities.

The same is true of the "moral luck" concept. The only way to judge the badness of a decision is to review it in comparison with the actual and potential outcomes based on analogy. If someone has a few drinks and runs into another car and kills someone, that's a definitive outcome. We know that action could lead to the death of a person because it did. We cannot know that about a situation where someone drove off into the bushes.

Driving intoxicated on two miles of country backroads at two o' clock in the morning, while not a good idea, is less of a threat to cause negative outcome than driving while intoxicated through a crowded residential area in the middle of the day. The law can judge and punish people for raising the potential for pain or injury, as is the case with reckless endangerment or reckless driving, but cannot judge an action as having led to a specific outcome. In other words, a drunk driver cannot be charged with vehicular manslaughter but can be charged with raising the statistical risk that harm would come to someone.

Regarding resistance against authority, particularly when governmental authority seeks to cause something as serious as a war: The question for the individual, then, must be this: "When is resistance really warranted?" When does refusing to go to war become a brave decision rather than an act of cowardice? If something truly threatens the nation in which one lives, then military service would seem to be a necessity. War proponents tend to accuse conscientious objectors of insincerely wanting to avoid being blown up in some foreign land, while war protestors tend to accuse the perpetrators of war as being for it for insincere reasons.

The George W. Bush administration, for example, proclaimed safety from weapons of mass destruction and the imposition of constitutional government to be the goals of the 2003 invasion of Iraq. Opponents of the war declared this to be insincere, with the real purpose of the war being to secure the Iraqi oil fields. This seems unlikely; wars get fought for ideologies and things like oil get secured in the process, not the other way around.

The charge of insincerity sometimes results in the development of conspiracy theories; the stated purpose of something hides the real and nefarious purpose. Who killed JFK? Did FDR know that the Japanese intended to bomb Pearl Harbor? Those kinds of questions assume a hidden purpose behind the insincere front of official governmental reports. If subordinates respond to real insincerity from authority with cynicism, then individuals who create false insincerity from authority do so from a sense of paranoia.

Conspiracy theories get bubbled up from a cauldron of paranoia and logic; depending upon the idea that if something looks designed, then it must be or that if a group benefits from something, then that group must have masterminded it. If Lyndon Johnson benefited, for example, from the assassination of JFK, then he must have caused it. If FDR wanted to enter into World War II despite a reluctant American populace, and the bombing of

Pearl Harbor allowed him to do that, then he must have let it occur. These are but two examples; genuine purveyors of paranoia stir a lot more into the pot.

This all ties in with the ultimate aim of psychology: to eliminate insincerity with the self. Self-actualization, a goal for psychologists in the same way that nirvana is for Buddhists, consists of knowing oneself perfectly and realizing the underlying reasons for one's behavior. At one level, the notion makes sense. All modern studies of Sigmund Freud tend to treat the man and his work with the same tone: he founded psychology but also falsified case histories and tried to pass off mystical ponderings as science. Freud scholars range their critiques on a spectrum between fraud and founding genius.

Freud thought that our self-images, based as they were/are on suppressed memories and urges, is itself insincere. He pushed this revolutionary insight into revolting territory by proposing that boys sexually lust for the mother, but because society frowns upon these urges and others, those emotions get buried and fester into the unconscious. The disjunction between the cognitive self-image and the buried desires creates insincerity within the self. The greater the insincerity, the more debilitating the psychological disorder becomes.

Suppressed emotions lie, as do ghosts, witches, and the Holy Trinity, beyond the evidence collecting powers of science. The very nature of a suppressed emotion indicates its hidden nature. When evidence is found for something that had previously been taken on faith (belief without evidence), then the thing ceases to require faith anymore. If a suppressed desire comes out into the open, it ceases to be suppressed.

Despite all this, clearly Freud got onto something with his notions of suppression. Although known for his case studies, his masterwork is *Civilization and Its Discontents* (1930). In the vein of the Enlightenment philosophers and the romantics, Freud notes that civilization itself alienates people and can cause psychological trauma and disorders.

One point of contention must be raised here: genetic evidence indicates that civilization cannot cause a disorder, but it might make disorders worse. Would a schizophrenic be happier and less consumed by symptoms in a pre-civilized society? Is it possible that hunter-gatherer societies could be healthier environments for people on the autism spectrum disorder than modern civilization?

According to Freud, all adult neuroses develop in part from internalized childhood angst. He got sidetracked by a fascination with repressed sexuality, but when connected with his thoughts about civilization, these two theories make sense. Babies come out of the womb with the same DNA as our pre-civilized forebears. We must adapt the presentations of those genes, through culture (the primary means of which are parenting and education), and this causes psychic pain.

Children quickly learn not to touch certain things, to behave, to stop screaming or throwing tantrums. Or, rather, they don't learn but face punishments over and over from adults who try to adapt them to a life indoors. Anthropological evidence might destroy any romantic notions about the hunter-gatherer lifestyle, but surely children raised in an environment without sharp edges, constant television chatter, and parents who busied themselves paying bills online fared better emotionally than modern suburban children.

Punishments don't change internal thoughts or behaviors; that's not the purpose. Instead, punishments teach children that certain behaviors should never get expressed in public. Sexual desires, and especially homosexual behavior, once brought public condemnation and legal recrimination. Men and women who felt those desires pressed them down, or found outlets in secret locations.

That insincerity brought an anxiety that, when applied en masse, eventually led to a cultural movement of attitudinal change. In an era of open sexuality, Freud's insights seem dusty, but at the time sexual repression of some sort may have defined the psychic inner life of generations of Europeans.

Might we describe parenting as "the raising of little hunter-gatherers in civilization"? No wonder the difficulties and costs become so overwhelming that so many young people the world over simply decided not to. The whole idea of family life with children—all those tedious birthday parties and hard seats in the soccer stands—looks like insincere public martyrdom for no cause at all.

In 1963, Betty Friedan wrote the following words to open *The Feminine Mystique*:

> The Problem lay buried, unspoken, for many years in the minds of American women. It was a strange stirring, a sense of dissatisfaction, a yearning that women suffered in the middle of the twentieth century in the United States. Each suburban wife struggled with it alone. As she made beds, shopped for groceries, matched slipcover material, ate peanut butter sandwiches with her children, chauffeured Cub Scouts and Brownies, lay beside her husband at night—she was afraid to ask ever of herself the silent question—"Is this all?" (2013 [1963], 1)

Friedan wrote only one brilliant passage; the rest of the book tediously repeats the conceit in different ways, but it proved to be enough to start a new feminist revolution. Her words made white housewives across the country question their sincerity with themselves. Then, those who decided they wanted more than peanut butter sandwiches and slipcover shopping, realized that society needed to offer more opportunities. Friedan got it right; psychological revolutions must come before societal revolutions, and her words touched the minds of American women just as the Pill touched their lips.

According to the writers who contributed essays to *Selfish, Shallow, and Self-Absorbed: Sixteen Writers on the Decision Not to Have Kids* (2015), child-raising is insincere in the sense that parents do not really want to do it, but see it as a necessary life stage. Those who have children do so because they worry that to not have children constitutes a sin against society, or they simply worry about missing out on something.

The same charge of insincerity could be aimed back at the childless; denial of one's biological destiny cannot come without some pain. However, measuring the regret of childlessness against the constant exhaustion and expense of parenting, one wonders whose accusations hold the most truth. Do all people become parents because they fear the regret of not becoming one will be more poignant than the pain of having them?

Most people love their kids. No doubt the cute pictures posted on Facebook come from a sincere place in the heart, but for many members of a new generation, family life looks insincere. What sounds better at 2 a.m., a shriek from the crib or the pulsing beat of a dance club? Does sitting on a bench and watching barely coordinated children kick/throw/chase/shoot balls really beat a late breakfast and cappuccino? What's wrong with reading silently and taking a painting class instead? Isn't living selfishly a sincerer form of life?

Philosophize on the question of "why have kids?" for a while, and the question leads to a singular conclusion: becoming a parent is a lifestyle choice. Why would we try to "cure" something like autism or Down syndrome if that was not the case?

Parents tend to want a healthy child that will live a relatively normal life and eventually provide grandchildren; a child that requires life-long care simply seems like too much of a burden for most people. We tend to think of children as lifestyle commodities anyway, which explains the prevalence of anxiety-ridden parents who hover over children for fear that the kid might get hurt (broken like a toy) or stolen.

The latter fear, which causes too many children to have to stay too close to parental control, gets implanted with capitalism. The thinking is that if a child contains value for the parent then the child must be valuable to others, which she is not. Relatively few children ever face kidnapping from strangers, and vastly more suffer from the diabetes and mental atrophy that comes from a life lived for too long indoors.

No one suffers from society's insincerity more than pregnant women. In 2008, Sarah Palin ran on the Republican presidential ticket with John McCain. Her young child at that time, a product of an over-forty pregnancy, possessed the chromosome mutation that presents as Down syndrome. This brings up a question: Would it be possible for a woman to be on a presidential ticket if her child had Down syndrome that was more likely linked to alcohol and drug abuse during the pregnancy?

A bunch of factors can increase the "risk" that a child will be born with Down syndrome. These include drug abuse, alcohol abuse, and becoming pregnant later in life. If babies with Down syndrome are something that society would like to avoid, then engaging in any of those risky actions should carry some type of societal penalty. No one shamed Palin for getting pregnant at a late age and no one should have, but should her actions be considered ethically different from drinking or drugging while pregnant? Drinking and drugging are choices, but so is becoming pregnant after thirty-five.

One take would be said that there's nothing wrong with Down syndrome children, so they should be celebrated no matter the means by which they were created. This would be fine, but again, try to imagine a scenario where a governor of a state drank heavily while pregnant, gave birth to a child with Down syndrome, and ended up on a presidential ticket.

Society might be illogical more than insincere, but it raises the idea that for every "congratulations" uttered to the parents of a child with a severe disability a silent "glad it's not me" gets whispered in the mind; perhaps the same happens when the voluntarily childless celebrate the birth of healthy children to others.

One should stay away from all social media at all times; the shaming refrains that get written in the anonymous comments section reads too much like a scripting of the self-hate that tortures the depressed. Yet, who could call incognito social media chatter insincere?

Anonymity contributes to the likelihood of sincerity; only the desire to appear as a certain kind of person among others prevents us from shouting out what we think at all times. In fact, it might be possible to define individuals with a certain kind of autism as "people with an insincerity deficiency," as they are unable to navigate what a social environment might require.

It could very well be that people tend to produce children for insincere reasons; it seems normal, they want to present themselves as parents, they want to make their own parents happy by giving them grandchildren, so the actual "work" of parenting gets limited. A massive industry exists that caters less to children than to the needs of lazy parents.

Sugary cereals and breakfast bars routinely get served to kids who need bacon, eggs, and whole grains. Cable television provides round-the-clock hypnotism; SpongeBob will keep your rug rat in place for an hour or so while you get the floors vacuumed. Video games will keep your adolescent docile in his room until the hormones making him act out settle down a little. If all you wanted was to haul a child out for Christmas morning or the occasional social media post, then it's perfect.

The problem is that this generates people who expect to be in the mode of "customer" all the time. Customers don't like to be pushed too hard; they like to get rewards for little effort. Schools exist to give out good grades and self-esteem. Students are asked to think of fifty different uses for a paperclip not because this is useful, but because it's more fun than trying to understand how ionization works.

The whole system, designed to placate customers, takes on a surreal insincerity. No one bloviates like the Fox News crowd, but rightists should be listened to when they decry the downfall of the American university. When students view the university as an arena to play out their social-justice fantasies, and when students create an identity for themselves that gets attached to a vague historical grievance, and then use that to bully the white power structure with their own liberal words, the end result is that no one goes to the library.

When students, most of them African American, took over Evergreen University in Washington State in 2017 over the issue of racism on campus, cell phone footage of the protests looked like film reels of Mao's Cultural Revolution. What drove the protesters into fits of screaming and inarticulate rage? The previous year, many African American students left campus in a "blackout" to protest institutional racism. No one questioned this; but in 2017, they demanded that white people leave in a "whiteout." This looked less like sensitivity training and more like bullying to one biology professor, and he dared say so.

One wonders how such a mild rebuke led to the sit-ins, shouting, cursing, bullying, and general terrorizing of faculty. One angry young women shouted "Whiteness is the most violent system to ever fucking breathe!" and received cheers; emotional inflection wins out over grammatical correctness in these kinds of situations, and even when language fails to perform its most basic function of conveying information, the insincerity could be felt. The point of these protests, likely, had nothing to do with racism but with establishing power against the weakest of opponents—the administration at a liberal arts college.

Nothing speaks to this trend like the so-called trigger warnings created by some professors to warn sensitive students that classroom materials might connect with something negative in their own lives and therefore "trigger" some kind of trauma. Rather than pile another learned condemnation on this (over-forty political commentators of all political factions find horror in trigger warnings), it's probably more disturbing to point out that no one made the connection of "trigger" warnings with Shakespeare's *Hamlet*.

Prince Hamlet, having left university life in Germany, returns home to Denmark. There, he finds that his father, the king, died by mysterious means. Hamlet's uncle Claudius now ruled as king, and to make matters more complicated, Claudius and Hamlet's mother, Gertrude, now slept together as man and wife.

The dead king's ghost haunts the castle, revealing information about his demise that drives Hamlet eventually mad. Hamlet's Uncle Claudius, goes the ghost's story, killed his sleeping brother by pouring poison into his ear.

Information passed on by ghosts might or might not be reliable. Hamlet himself seems to question whether he believes in the villainy of Claudius and so connives a plan to "trigger" the king's guilt with an insincere "The play's the thing. Wherein I'll catch the conscience of the king," as he arrays his players into a performance called *The Mousetrap*. Evil King Claudius must sit and watch a recreation of his (presumably) darkest personal moment when one character murders another by pouring poison into his ear.

Triggered, Claudius suffers a bout of mania and penitence. He avoids death only because, during his guilty prayer (is there anything less sincere than a sudden penitent), Hamlet fears that stabbing the man might send him to heaven. Hamlet, by using the tools of insincerity, tears apart the entire insincere court around him with sincere and murderous rage. We like Hamlet, we do, because he asserts himself as The Man rather than suffering a secondary status and living as a meek thing under the authority of a usurping king.

In some ways, the students of Evergreen College (and their brethren at Reed College, who can be seen on YouTube bullying their way into a lecture hall, holding protest signs, speaking nonsense with prep-school diction, and taking over an otherwise boring course on Mediterranean history for some reason or another) are simply performing insincere experiments on society.

Harold Garfinkel (1917–2011), turned the common prank into a scholarly discipline by developing ethnomethodology. The primary tool of the ethnomethodologist is the *breaching experiment*, which involves the breaking of a social norm for the purpose of discovering what the social norm actually was. If someone sings show tunes while sitting in the waiting room of an oil lube joint and receives an inordinate amount of attention for doing so, then one can determine that singing show tunes in that environment may not be socially normal.

Mostly, this is just an excuse for psychology/sociology undergrads to screw around with working people, but the concept revels in insincerity. Breaching experiments might be called anti-experiments in the sense that they turn people who are minding their own businesses into the subjects of experimentation for the purpose of finding out something about society rather than something about them as people.

Insincere displays of the abnormal highlight the sincerity of the normal.

In the nineteenth century, the Russian *intelligentsia* refuted insincerity, seeing it as a tool of the czar. Russians missed the developments that restructured Western civilization during the postmedieval period. From the thirteenth century until the sixteenth century, the Russians suffered from Mongol dominance, something that sapped the economic energy from the society and wrenched Russia's culture eastward.

This meant that the Russian Empire missed the Renaissance, missed the Reformation, and missed the Scientific Revolution. No Russian explorers sailed the Atlantic, and serfdom kept Russia's economy in a feudal and agricultural state. The serfs, lice ridden and kept in ignorance, did not seem to mind. It was the sons and daughters of the nobility—who went to the university and encountered the revolutionary ideals of classical liberalism—who sought change.

This led to a strange psychological and political revolution since would-be revolutionaries (called *narodniks*), quickly found that they could not radicalize the serfs into rebellion. Instead, the revolutionaries could change themselves. This led to an anti-insincerity inner cult, something described by Aileen Kelly in the introduction to the Penguin Classics 2008 version of Isaiah Berlin's *Russian Thinkers*:

> This yearning for absolutes was one source of that notorious consistency which, as Berlin observes, was the most striking characteristic of Russian thinkers—their habit of taking ideas and concepts to their most extreme, even absurd, conclusion: to stop before the ultimate consequences of one's reasoning was seen as moral cowardice, insufficient commitment to truth. (Kelly in Berlin 2008 [1978], xxvii)

From this philosophical concept came Lenin, Trotsky, and Stalin, each of whom asked himself "what is to be done?" and found answers in the use of terror.

In a society of equals, otherwise known as a democratic republic, insincere flattery of power becomes less important. The ability to use intelligent insincerity as a means of exercising influence defines much of American history. The most ingenious practitioner of the art pulled his swindle so well that all Americans continue to view his political trick with reverence and awe.

James Madison, the author of the Constitution and the fourth president, did not see the need for a document that enumerated the rights of the people. Madison believed that if the Constitution failed to forbid something, then the people should assume on the side of freedom.

The anti-federalists, led by James Mason, opposed the Constitution on the grounds that it must contain a bill of rights like the English had enjoyed since 1689. Madison thought this a silly request and rightfully so. Imagine taking a group of kids to a playground. You show them the rules; they say "no jumping off the slides. No pushing. No punching." Then you say, "Go play, kids!"

Instead of playing, the children cross their arms and stare at you grumpily. They don't trust you and want a guarantee that they can go down the slides. You become incredulous. "You can already go down the slides. If this doesn't say you can't do it, then you can." No good. They are grumpy, they need a snack, and they want the guarantee.

You shrug and amend the sign to say that "the right to go down the slide shall not be infringed." They want the same guarantee for the swing sets and monkey bars. There's no talking to them, so you write it down. Finally, exasperated with the whole stupid process you write a final amendment "and if it doesn't say you can't do it, then you can." This last amendment makes all the other amendments completely pointless and therefore insincere.

Our vaunted Bill of Rights, hanging in reverence in every government building and piously defended by both the National Rifle Association and the American Civil Liberties Union, should be seen as nothing but a relic of Madison's manipulative genius. "You want a bill of rights? Here's your bill of rights." He seems to be saying this to the anti-federalists. However, when he got to the end of his enumerative work, he wrote: "The powers not delegated to the United States by the Constitution, nor prohibited by it to the States, are reserved to the states respectively, or to the people." In other words, if the Constitution does not say you can't do it, then you can.

What, now, could the anti-federalists do? Madison gave them what they asked for without changing a thing from his original vision; the whole point of the Bill of Rights was not what it seemed. Madison wrote the Constitution and sent it to the states for ratification, and when they sent it back, he pretended to listen but changed nothing. The Bill of Rights might as well read "Thanks so much for your feedback."

KEY POINTS

- The idea of insincerity within the self is a key idea of psychology. The goal of psychotherapy, for the individual, might be described as the attempt to attain sincerity between one's expressed and hidden thoughts and desires.
- Popular culture provides several examples of people being "tricked" through insincere setups into revealing serious character flaws. However, most of us likely exist in a state of moral equivalence until we choose a course of action and then decide that we were "always for" or "always against" something.
- As a branch of the feminist movement begun by Betty Friedan, a new life philosophy that considers parenting to be an act of insincerity has some vocal and articulate proponents. Our thinking about pregnancy and motherhood is corrupted by illogical and insincere thinking.

- The desire to eradicate insincerity is behind much of Russia's radical political history.
- James Madison wrote the Bill of Rights purely to shut up the anti-federalists, and the Tenth Amendment renders the other nine completely pointless. History's most insincere document hangs in every hallowed political hall in the United States.

Conclusion

Of all the cultural examples of insincerity, my favorite is from the 1939 *Wizard of Oz* movie. No one understood insincerity better than the Wizard himself. A plump old man, he cloaked himself in mystery and power and terrified Dorothy, the Tin Man, the Lion, and the Scarecrow to such a great extent that they failed to see the central flaw in the story's reasoning: if the Wizard possessed such terrifying power, then why didn't he just do away with the Wicked Witch of the West himself? Had Dorothy et al. possessed just a little more cognitive power they might have wondered why the Wizard claimed just enough power to grant a wish but not enough power to plant a witch.

The dog, Toto, ultimately, figures this out for Dorothy and her band, but this is where the Wizard reveals his true talent: he's a master of insincerity studies. He points out to the Scarecrow that plenty of people get by fine with no brains and that a good many are in universities; they just have something that he doesn't: a university degree.

Did anybody else catch how subversive the Wizard's speech to the Lion was? He tells the lion that running away from danger is wisdom, not cowardice, and that "Back where I come from, we have men who are called 'heroes.' Once a year they take their fortitude out of mothballs and parade it down the Main Street of the city and they have no more courage than you have. But they have one thing that you haven't got: a medal."

The Wizard sees how false honors turn the brainless into the intelligent and the cowardly into the brave.

Overall, insincerity possesses a bad reputation, and it is certainly the case that an excessive use of it can spoil relationships. If a boss, colleague, or spouse only makes time to talk with you when they want something then they become "transparent." The word *transparent* itself indicates the nature of insincerity; people can see through the stated purpose of the interaction to the real.

Yet, treating insincerity itself as a negative thing without further examination provides little in the way of insight into its form and functions. Hopefully, this book raised the question of "what's so great about sincerity?" in addition to examining insincerity.

For professors and teachers, it might be interesting to challenge students to find their own examples of insincerity in culture. Show students examples and then direct them to find their own course. Readers of this book can come up with dozens or hundreds of cultural examples of insincerity that received no commentary here. Good. This is not a doctoral dissertation, not an exhaustive study, but a framework for understanding insincerity's history and function in society.

Probably, too much contact with insincerity can poison a person's psychological state. To constantly bump up against a power structure that cares not at all leads to the building up of frustrations. Failure to act on those frustrations and the acceptance of lowered status eventually gets in your bones and makes you something less than what you might be.

The Stoics of ancient Greece understood this, and so they invented a philosophy about the self and interaction with society. Sincerity counted for more than the material goods and popularity that insincerity brought. People still divide themselves up in these camps, although one suspects that some people only become martyrs for sincerity when their insincere attempts to gain riches and popularity fail. No one, in truth, makes the decision wholly either way. The Stoic ideal of an entirely sincere man exists only in Platonic form; we might try to limit our insincere responses but to eliminate them entirely would be to live a life more devoted to an ideal than to other human beings.

Being social creatures, insincerity helps us hold relationships, and therefore society, together when used in small doses. Sincerity in too great a measure leads to self-destructive behavior—martyrdom and the like. In normal societal doses, sincerity probably holds Western civilization together.

The people who smile when taking your order, who show up to work on time, who park cars, or paint houses, or mow lawns, these people make a sincere effort to do a job well when given it keeps society moving along. These are not little things, and they deserve to be repaid with the courtesy of politeness. Those at the top of the power structure might do well to recognize this and respond to the legitimate needs of workers with a sincerity given back in the same measure.

Teachers and professors should always be careful when employing the "cultural studies are good for society" notion in the classroom. As Harold Bloom has written, one cannot study the Western canon for any outward reason but only for "the proper use of one's own solitude" (1994, 28). This statement should hang over the gates of every liberal arts university and be the motto of every English department. Any claim that the study of the humanities will do more than enhance one's own solitary reading and living experience enters into trouble when subjected to cold analysis.

Still, as a method of enhancing understanding, it's always a good idea to help students see that the kind of human relationships that one encounters in literature can also be seen on MTV or social media. That connection enriches the experience of both modern culture and the study of past culture and provides an interesting means to gain the interest of students.

Ultimately, a deeper understanding of insincerity might help us all to better conceive of when it should be applied and when it should not. Western civilization holds a special place for the sincere rebel, while Eastern societies prefer insincere obedience. Is the view of insincerity a point of important cultural division? Maybe, but to make too much of the idea might be insincere in itself.

Readers, particularly subordinates who encounter insincerity in their daily working lives, might like some advice about how to deal with insincerity. My advice comes from Cicero, not the real Cicero, but the fictional character based on the real Cicero that the novelist Robert Harris created for his trilogy about ancient Rome. In the first book of that series, *Imperium*, Harris has Cicero say:

> Sometimes . . . if you find yourself stuck in politics, the thing to do is start a fight—start a fight, even if you do not know how you are going to win it, because it is only when a fight is on, and everything is in motion, that you can see your way through. (2006, 37)

Nothing upends an insincere situation like raw emotion, and assertive (but not aggressive) anger can sometimes throw off a bureaucratic apparatus that operates only when subordinates are intimidated into passiveness. That passiveness, that fear, can take away from your own sense of your humanity. In those situations, it's better to start a sincere fight than to subject yourself to humiliation.

The real Cicero, of course, picked a fight with Marc Antony after the death of Caesar. Antony's soldiers hacked off Cicero's head and hands, then Antony ordered that both of them be nailed to the doorway over the forum. The thuggish Antony considered the hands, in particular, to be trophies because they had so often written against him. Power is power; it always has been, so be careful.

Antony, by the way, chose to fight against his brother-in-law and co-emperor Octavian because he sincerely loved Cleopatra. He ended up falling on a sword and dying slowly for sincerity . . . and so the story goes on.

References

Andersen, Hans Christian. *The Complete Fairy Tales.* San Diego: Canterbury Classics, 2014.
Bauer, Susan Wise. *The History of the Ancient World: From the Earliest Accounts Until the Fall of Rome.* New York: Norton, 2007.
Berlin, Isaiah. *Russian Thinkers.* London: Penguin Classics, 2008. Originally published in 1978.
Bloom, Harold. *The Western Canon: The Books and Schools of the Ages.* New York: Houghton Mifflin Harcourt, 1994.
Boethius. *The Consolation of Philosophy.* London: Penguin Classics, reprinted 1999.
Darwin, Charles. "The Descent of Man." In *From So Simple a Beginning: The Four Great Books of Charles Darwin.* New York: Norton, 2006.
Daum, Meghan, ed. *Selfish, Shallow, and Self-Absorbed: Sixteen Writers on the Decision Not to Have Kids.* New York: Picador, 2015.
Deleuze, Gilles and Guattari, Felix. *Anti-Oedipus: Capitalism and Schizophrenia.* London: Penguin Classics Press, 1977.
Diamond, Jared. *The Third Chimpanzee: The Evolution and Future of the Human Animal.* New York: Harper Perennial, 1992.
Douglass, Frederick. *Narrative of the Life of Frederick Douglass, an American Slave.* London: Penguin Classics, reprinted 1986. Originally published in 1845.
Edmonds, David, and Nigel Warburton. *Philosophy Bites Again: 27 Leading Thinkers on 27 Intriguing Topics.* Oxford: Oxford University Press, 2014.
Evans, Richard. *The Third Reich in Power.* New York: Penguin Group, 2006.
Feinstein, John. *A Season on the Brink: A Year with Bob Knight and the Indiana Hoosiers.* New York: Macmillan, 1986.
Flynn, Gillian. *Gone Girl.* New York: Broadway Books, 2014.
Foxe, John. *Book of Martyrs: Select Narratives.* Oxford: Oxford University Press, reprinted 2009.
Freud, Sigmund. *Civilization and Its Discontents.* New York: Norton, 1961. Originally published in 1930.
Friedan, Betty. *The Feminine Mystique: 50th Anniversary Edition.* New York: Norton, 2013. Originally published in 1963.
Gessen, Masha. *Perfect Rigor: A Genius and the Mathematical Breakthrough of the Century.* New York: Houghton Mifflin, 2009.
Goffman, Erving. *The Presentation of Self in Everyday Life.* New York: Bantam Doubleday Dell, 1956.
Greer, Thomas H., and Gavin Lewis. *A Brief History of the Western World.* New York: Harcourt College Publishers, 2002.

Gribbin, John. *The Scientists: A History of Science Told through the Lives of Its Greatest Inventors.* New York: Random House Trade Paperbacks, 2004.
Harris, Robert. *Imperium: A Novel of Ancient Rome.* New York: Pocket Books, 2006.
Harvard Rhetorical Society. http://www.hcs.harvard.edu/~rhetoric/luther.htm.
Hawking, Stephen. *On the Shoulders of Giants: The Great Works of Physics and Astronomy.* Philadelphia: Running Press Book Publishers, 2002.
Heller, Joseph. *Catch-22: 50th Anniversary Edition.* New York: Simon & Schuster, reprinted 2011. Originally published in 1961.
Herodotus. *The Histories.* London: Penguin Classics, reprinted 2003.
Hitchens, Christopher. *Hitch-22: A Memoir.* New York: Twelve, 2010.
Hobbes, Thomas. *Leviathan.* London: Penguin Classics, reprinted 1985.
Hunt, Morton. *The Story of Psychology.* New York: Anchor Books, 2009.
Keizer, Garrett. *Getting Schooled: The Reeducation of an American Teacher.* New York: Henry Holt, 2014.
Kimmel, Michael. *Guyland: The Perilous World Where Boys Become Men.* New York: HarperCollins, 2008.
Lapidus, Ira M. *A History of Islamic Societies.* Cambridge: Cambridge University Press, 1988.
Locke, John. "An Essay Concerning Human Understanding." In *The English Philosophers from Bacon to Mill*, edited by Edwin A. Burt, 253–424. New York: Modern Library, 1994.
MacCulloch, Diarmaid. *Christianity: The First Three Thousand Years.* New York: Viking, 2009.
Machiavelli, Niccolo. *The Prince.* London: Penguin Classics, 2003.
Madariaga, Isabel D. *Ivan the Terrible.* New Haven, CT: Yale University Press, 2006.
Narayan, R. K. *The Guide.* London: Penguin Classics, 1956, reprinted 2006.
Neely, Kim. *Five against One: The Pearl Jam Story.* New York: Penguin Books, 1998.
Nietzsche, Friedrich. *Twilight of the Idols/The Anti-Christ.* London: Penguin Classics, 1990.
Norwich, John Julius. *Byzantium: The Apogee.* New York: Knopf, 1996.
Orwell, George. *1984.* New York: Signet Classics, reprinted 1990. Originally published in 1949.
Pagden, Anthony. *The Enlightenment and Why It Still Matters.* New York: Random House, 2013.
Plato. *The Last Days of Socrates.* London: Penguin Classics, 1954, reprinted 2003.
Plutarch. *On Sparta.* London: Penguin Classics, 1988.
Procopius. *The Secret History.* London: Penguin Classics, reprinted 1966.
Radzinksy, Edvard. *Stalin: The First In-Depth Biography Based on Explosive New Documents from Russia's Secret Archives.* New York: Anchor Books, 1996.
Rorabaugh, W. J. *The Alcoholic Republic: An American Tradition.* Oxford: Oxford University Press, 1979.
Rousseau, Jean Jacques. *Emile; or, On Education.* London: Penguin Classics, 2007.
———. *The Confessions.* London: Penguin Classics, reprinted 1953.
———. "The Social Contract." In *The European Philosophers from Descartes to Nietzsche*, edited by Monroe C. Beardsley, 321–69. New York: Modern Library, 2002.
Rubenstein, Richard. *Aristotle's Children: How Christians, Muslims, and Jews Rediscovered Ancient Wisdom and Illuminated the Middle Ages.* Orlando, FL: Harcourt, 2003.
Salinger, J. D. *The Catcher in the Rye.* New York: First Bay Paperback, 2001.
Schumacher, Julie. *Dear Committee Members.* New York: Anchor Books, 2015.
Shields, David, and Shane Salerno. *Salinger.* New York: Simon & Schuster, 2013.
Sophocles. *The Three Theban Plays:* Antigone, Oedipus the King, Oedipus at Colonus. London: Penguin Classics, reprinted 1984.
Taylor, Telford. *The Anatomy of the Nuremberg Trials: A Personal Memoir.* New York: Skyhorse Publishing, 2013.
Thody, Phillip, and Howard Read. *Introducing Sartre.* Cambridge: Icon Books, 1998.
Twain, Mark. *The Adventures of Tom Sawyer.* London: Penguin Classics, 2006.
von Goethe, Johann Wolfgang. *The Sorrows of Young Werther.* London: Penguin Classics, 1989. Originally published in 1774.

Weatherford, Jack. *Genghis Khan and the Making of the Modern World*. New York: Three Rivers Press, 2004.
Wollstonecraft, Mary. *A Vindication of the Rights of Woman*. London: Penguin Classics, 2004. Originally published in 1792.
Wu, Duncan. *Romanticism: An Anthology*. Chichester: Wiley-Blackwell, 2012.
X, Malcolm, as told to Alex Haley. *The Autobiography of Malcolm X*. New York: Ballantine Books, 1989.

About the Author

Chris Edwards is a veteran teacher of World History and Advanced Placement World History at a public high school in the Midwest and is the author of several books, including the five-volume *Connecting the Dots in World History* series published by R&L Education. He is a frequent contributor to *Skeptic* magazine on the topics of law, logic, psychology, theoretical physics, and education. Chris directs a generous grant from the Scientech Foundation for a Summer Institute for Math and Science teachers through Ball State University. His teaching methodology and scholarship have been published by the National Council for Social Studies (NCSS) and the National Council for History Education. He has presented his teaching methodology to a national audience through a two-part webinar series hosted by the NCSS.